SILICON VALLEY GIRL

May Ijisesan

A MEMOIR OF AMBITION,
IDENTITY, AND FAITH

This book or any portion thereof may not be reproduced or used in any manner whatsoever without the express written permission of the author/publisher except for the use of brief quotations in a book review.

Copyright © 2025 Mayowa Ijisesan

Paperback ISBN - 978-1-7375968-3-7

Cover Design by Temi Ijisesan | IG @dawn_of_art

Scripture quotations marked NKJV are taken from the New King James Version®. Copyright © 1982 by Thomas Nelson. Used by permission. All rights reserved.

Scripture quotations marked AMPC are taken from the Amplified® Bible, Classic Edition (AMPC), Copyright © 1954, 1958, 1962, 1964, 1965, 1987 by The Lockman Foundation. Used by permission. All rights reserved.

Scripture quotations marked NLT are taken from the Holy Bible, NEW LIVING TRANSLATION, copyright © 1996, 2004, 2015 by Tyndale House Foundation. Used by permission of Tyndel House Publishers, Inc.,Carol Stream, Illinois 60188. All rights reserved.

Dedication

To everyone who's ever felt like the "only one" in the room—
Don't shrink to fit in. You were born to stand out in your uniqueness.

Table of Contents

Dedication iii

Introduction 1

Chapter 1
Intentional Beginnings 3

Chapter 2
Coming to America 13

Chapter 3
Life at Cornell 23

Chapter 4
Silicon Valley 33

Chapter 5
Marriage, Miracles, and Trying Times 45

Chapter 6
Notable Miracles 59

Chapter 7
Mum at Work 67

Chapter 8
The only (Black) Woman in the Room 75

Chapter 9
Sacrificing Isaac: Leaving for Full-Time Ministry 87

Chapter 10
Getting Isaac Back 95

Chapter 11
A Call to Consecration 101

Chapter 12
Heart at Work 109

Chapter 13
The Christian at Work 119

Chapter 14
Conclusion 127

Acknowledgements 129

About the Author 131

Introduction

In today's ever-evolving world, careers are no longer just a means of livelihood—they are reflections of our values, passions, and purpose. This book invites you into my journey, one where professional ambition intersects deeply with faith, family, and personal identity. From Silicon Valley's fast-paced tech hubs to transformative moments in ministry, I've navigated the nuanced terrain of balancing vision with conviction. Through every season, I've come to believe that our careers aren't just about achievement, they are about fulfilling a higher calling and making a meaningful impact in the world.

When I stepped into my first role as a software engineer at Altera Corporation in 1999, I felt a mix of excitement and uncertainty. As one of the few Black women in Silicon Valley at the time, the challenges I faced extended beyond technical skills. I had to navigate cultural isolation, battle self-doubt, and confront subtle yet persistent biases. But those early experiences became powerful teachers. They shaped my resilience, fueled my pursuit of excellence, and taught me the value of leading with authenticity.

At the heart of my career journey is the principle of consecration; the intentional decision to dedicate my ambitions and work to a greater purpose. Consecration isn't about preaching at work. It's about infusing our decisions, relationships, and goals with the values of faith, integrity, and service. When I left a flourishing tech career in California to help start a church in Chicago, it wasn't just a career pivot. It was a step of obedience, sacrifice, and trust—one that changed the trajectory of my life and deepened my understanding of what it means to live a life of impact.

Throughout this memoir, one theme consistently rises to the surface: integrity. Integrity is more than doing what's right, but it's about being the same person in every room, whether you're leading a team, handling a crisis, or making a hard decision. It is the courage to stay rooted in your values, even when it's not easy. In both my corporate and ministerial work, I've seen how integrity doesn't just protect your reputation. It also strengthens your influence.

I also explore the very real pressures of comparison and competitive jealousy. It's easy to measure our worth by the success of others, especially in professional environments that thrive on metrics and accolades. I've felt those tugs. But I've also learned the freedom that comes from embracing your unique path that is shaped by divine purpose, distinct talents, and hard-won wisdom.

As you'll read in the chapters ahead, consecration doesn't mean abandoning excellence. In fact, it calls us to it. It means being diligent, adaptable, and always teachable. From my early days in Nigeria, shaped by my entrepreneurial mother and engineer father, to the academic rigor of the University of Oklahoma and Cornell University, and then into Silicon Valley, I've seen how discipline and structure lay the foundation for breakthroughs. And through every career shift, whether in business or ministry, I've discovered that excellence is not about being the best; it's about bringing your best, consistently.

This book is for anyone longing to align their career with their convictions. Whether you're just starting out, scaling the heights of your profession, or standing at a crossroads, I hope these stories and lessons resonate with you. My aim is to offer both inspiration and practical tools for navigating work with clarity, purpose, and faith.

Let's redefine what it means to thrive. Let's see our careers not just as ladders to climb, but as platforms for service. Let's believe that faith and ambition don't have to compete, but they can work together to build something lasting. Welcome to the journey of a consecrated career, where purpose, passion, and profession beautifully converge under divine guidance.

1

Intentional Beginnings

As the saying goes, "The childhood chose the man as the morning chose the day." It is impossible to separate my career journey from my childhood years.

My mother, Pamela Ibironke Adefolaju, has profoundly shaped the person I am today. Her nurturing instilled in me a passion for learning and personal growth, as well as the values of diligence and hard work. These qualities have not only advanced my career but have also defined my character as a woman.

My earliest recollections of my mom include images of her brown sedan, a Nissan Datsun, a popular model in Nigeria back then that has since been phased out. I vividly remember that brown car because she always had a box of fiction books in the trunk. My mother did not believe in idleness. You were either reading, doing a house chore, or resting. So, whenever I asked to visit a friend's house, especially during the holidays, that trunk would pop open and out would come a fresh batch of books that my mom suggested (actually insisted) that I read instead.

My mother was a very enterprising woman. She could keep fresh supplies of books coming our way because she owned a bookstore, Rontad Bookstore. And that wasn't even her day job. Her 9 to 5 was as a senior researcher and librarian at the National Institute for Horticultural Research (NIHORT). She didn't like to do much reading at home because her work required a lot of reading already. When she was home, she liked to relax and make sure we were gainfully occupied.

I grew up loving books. We had a library at home with volumes and volumes of books, which I later discovered was rare in Nigerian households at the time. I assumed everyone else got lost in a book over the weekend. Or everyone was doing their schoolwork or reading a book, even while preparing supper. We had a very regimented schedule that stayed the same, even during the weekend or over the holidays. She just ensured that we were constantly engaged in something productive.

Our days followed a schedule that, at the time, felt like clockwork—one that began at 5:30 a.m. with family prayers and transitioned seamlessly into chores. My responsibility was sweeping the carpeted living room, a daunting task, especially when the vacuum cleaner was on the fritz, which was often. So there I was, each morning, hunched over with a short broom better suited for the job, sweeping a living room that seemed to stretch endlessly into the dining area. It taught me grit long before I knew the word.

After chores, it was the usual morning rush—breakfast, uniforms, and out the door by 7 a.m. for a long commute through the traffic-laden streets of Ibadan. We were rarely late. Punctuality was expected, and somehow, we made it happen.

Afternoons had their own rhythm. After returning from school, typically between 3 and 4 p.m., we knew what came next—lunch and then 'settle down' time at 4:30 p.m. That phrase, unique to our household, meant one thing: go to your assigned desk and study. With six children in the house—including cousins—each of us had a designated desk. We didn't dare chat or mess around. The rule was simple and enforced: when you settled down, you stayed settled.

The evening unfolded in a similar cadence: study, dinner, a bit of television, and then another study session from 8 to 10 p.m. Family devotion followed, then bedtime by 10:30. Weekends gave us a small reprieve with a 7:30 a.m. wake-up, but the evening routines never changed. Church events were the only exception to our routine, and even then, those disruptions were few and far between. Faith and church attendance were not just important, they were non-negotiable pillars of our family life. Sunday services, midweek gatherings, and special programs were part of our regular rhythm.

By most standards, our daily routine might have seemed rigid, but my mother knew what she was doing. Her structure, her standards, and her unwavering belief in our potential set a foundation that propelled us forward. Among us are engineers, a triple-board-certified doctor, and a university professor. My mother wasn't just raising children, she was shaping futures. She had a blueprint that worked, and she followed it with unwavering conviction.

I spent countless hours at the library of my mother's workplace. During school holidays, when I wasn't working through the stacks of books she gave me, she would take me with her to the office. From the moment she clocked in to the moment she left, I sat at a desk, solving math problems, practicing grammar, and immersing myself in learning. For her, excellence wasn't optional. It was expected. And to her, it was perfectly natural that I wanted to excel too.

When my mother eventually closed her bookstore, Rontad Bookstore, it wasn't because she lacked vision. It was because the economic climate in Nigeria made it almost impossible to operate profitably. But her entrepreneurial spirit didn't fade. She simply channeled it into something new: a farm.

I grew up on an animal farm. We had everything from poultry to snails, rabbits to goats, even ducks and turkeys. She also ran a fishpond. But her boldest venture was her piggery, which was at one point, the third-largest in Ibadan. Each time it was devastated by a disease outbreak, she rebuilt. Twice. The third time, she chose to let it go, turning her focus instead to supporting my father during his illness.

My mother was, and still is, a maverick in my book. When I was admitted into my dream graduate program at Cornell and questioned whether we could afford it, she and my father didn't flinch. They assured me they would find a way, and they did. I arrived in the U.S. in 1995 with just enough for a year and a half of tuition, shared between my brother and me. We began by faith. And year after year, God provided. Eventually, my father paid for all three of our undergraduate and graduate degrees. My younger sister completed medical school in Nigeria and moved to the U.S. for residency and fellowships. It felt like the jar of oil that never ran dry.

My mother was instrumental in helping me raise children while managing a career and ministry. She had a gift for grounding me when I drifted, for reordering my priorities when I lost sight of what mattered. She encouraged me when I felt overwhelmed and reminded me of what was truly important.

While I wasn't nearly as organized as she was because my home didn't run like a naval ship, her influence helped me raise centered, grounded children.

She introduced my kids to what she called "settling down." At just five and six years old, she expected them to bring their Bibles and notebooks to church and take notes, even in adult services. Afterward, she'd ask to see what they had written. There was no room for idleness or distraction. She conducted devotions, prayed with them, and reinforced spiritual lessons with the same consistency that marked her approach to education. At first, it was an adjustment for them; learning to sit quietly, focus, and take notes at such a young age. But over time, it became a familiar rhythm, just as it had for me years earlier. What initially felt challenging eventually built discipline and attention, and a general disposition of discipline that still serves them today.

I vividly remember one semester when parenting felt especially demanding. My son was in middle school; my daughter was in upper elementary. I had missed two consecutive midweek services because I was buried under homework support. I assumed my mother, ever the champion of academic rigor, would understand. But when she called me from Philadelphia, where she was staying with my sister, her voice held no sympathy. "That's not how you were raised," she reminded me. "You went to church—even when it was inconvenient."

Her words landed. And they stuck. We adjusted. We found a way. And today, I'm grateful. My children are now in college, and despite their busy schedules, church is a priority. That training has carried forward.

Even though my mother passed much earlier than I would have ever wished, her legacy lives on in me and in the way I parent. She taught me that parenting isn't just about love. It's about vision, structure, and preparing your children for success. Her lessons still guide me, and her memory inspires me daily.

My mom will always be my hero.

I was fortunate to be raised by two extraordinary parents. My decision to pursue a career in technology was directly influenced by my father, Dr. Gabriel Olatunbosun Adefolaju.

While my mother's discipline and entrepreneurial spirit laid the groundwork for my growth, it was my father's quiet wisdom and steady encouragement that shaped my ambition and guided my professional aspirations.

One afternoon, while riding in his golden-brown Mercedes-Benz, we found ourselves stopped at a railroad crossing in Ibadan. As the long train passed, he turned to me and asked, "What do you want to be when you grow up?"

At the time, I was intrigued by the idea of aeronautical engineering. I knew little about the field except that it involved airplanes and required strong math skills which was something I had always excelled at. With a mix of excitement and nerves, I blurted out, "An aeronautical engineer."

My father, a civil engineer and one of Nigeria's leading minds in the field, looked at me with a calm, practical expression. Then he asked, "And how do you think you're going to practice that in Nigeria?" His tone wasn't dismissive, but it was realistic. Looking back, I'm grateful that he didn't discourage my dreams but redirected them. And importantly, he never once made me feel like I couldn't achieve something because I was a girl. His belief in my potential became one of the foundational pillars of my confidence, especially in rooms where I was the only woman.

I went on to gain admission to Obafemi Awolowo University in 1992, a year ahead of schedule. I had tested early, passed on the first try, and was admitted to study Electrical and Electronics Engineering, a path my father fully supported. He was proud, and I lived for moments that made him proud. His approval was a powerful motivator. I've often said that fathers play a critical role in shaping their daughters' sense of possibility, and mine certainly did. He anchored my ambitions in reason without ever dimming their light.

My father's influence extended far beyond my academic choices. His unwavering belief in my abilities inspired my confidence as a woman in tech. He modeled diligence and brilliance, solving complex engineering problems across Nigeria through his consulting firm. While my mother taught me how to work, my father showed me what it meant to excel. He didn't just teach math—he demonstrated mastery. He didn't just support our education—he invested in it wholeheartedly.

He never flaunted wealth, but he was steady in his provision. He built a modest but tasteful home, choosing substance over status. I never considered us wealthy, which made it even more surprising to realize later how far his quiet financial commitment stretched. He funded my undergraduate and graduate studies, as well as my siblings'. His support allowed us to dream boldly without being burdened by how we would pay for those dreams.

My father passed away several years after I got married, leaving a profound gap I only fully recognized years later.

After his death, it took me years to see how deeply his absence had affected me. In a church service four years following his passing, a guest preacher spoke about loss; how God can restore even the time we think we've lost. In that moment, it hit me. Without my father's voice cheering me on, I had quietly lowered the bar for myself. I had stopped reaching as far. I had settled. But that day, I made a decision: I would stop coasting. I would stretch again. I would keep aiming high—not because he was watching, but because his belief in me was still alive in the way I believed in myself.

My parents laid a solid foundation of faith, discipline, and ambition—values that have profoundly shaped my worldview. It was against this backdrop of family nurture and personal growth that I encountered someone who would further deepen and refine these values in ways I had never anticipated.

Many people don't know that I met my husband when I was a teenager. That moment changed the trajectory of my life, not just romantically, but spiritually and professionally. Let me tell you the story of how I met and fell in love with a boy who would become my husband, my partner in ministry, and one of the most influential voices in my journey.

It was my second year at Obafemi Awolowo University in Ile-Ife, Nigeria. I wasn't looking for love. I was likely on my way to the library when I bumped into a classmate walking in the opposite direction. Beside him was another young man who looked slightly older. My classmate paused to introduce us.

"Hello, Kunle," I said.

"Hello, Mayowa," he replied. "Meet my pastor, Pastor Kay."

I looked him over. He didn't look like any pastor I had known. He was young, too young, I thought, to be leading a fellowship. But this was OAU, where spiritual passion ran deep, and many young people were already stepping into ministry. He asked me a few simple questions, but I remember giving what I now recognize were rather odd answers. I was in a deeply zealous phase of my life, passionate about God but tangled in religious rigidity. What I had in abundance was zeal; what I lacked was clarity. That imbalance had started to pull me into spiritual discouragement.

As I would later learn, my answers caught Pastor Kay's attention, but not in the way I hoped. After we became friends, he told me his first thought after our conversation was, "That girl needs a lot of help."

A few months later, I walked into the campus fellowship he pastored. Something about it felt right. I stayed. Week after week, I listened to him teach the Word of God in a way I hadn't heard before; clear, compassionate, liberating. Without even realizing it, the heavy burden of religious striving began to lift. I no longer lived under a cloud of guilt or condemnation. I felt accepted, seen, and loved by God, not because of what I could do, but simply because I was His.

At first, I admired Pastor Kay's teaching. Then, I admired his leadership. He loved the fellowship members genuinely, and his humility was disarming. He was grounded, real, and remarkably down to earth. Slowly, that admiration turned into something deeper. I realized I had fallen in love with my pastor, and I didn't know what to do with that. It felt inappropriate, and I wrestled with guilt. I prayed for the feelings to go away. But they didn't.

God, however, had a plan. Before long, He spoke to Kayode too, confirming to him that I was His choice for him. Kay had noticed me, but he had kept his distance out of integrity. The fellowship was small, and he didn't want any perception of manipulation. But when God made it clear, he responded.

On September 1, 1994, he asked me to be his partner, not just in life, but in purpose. I said yes. And that yes has defined much of my life since.

Kayode was a pharmacy student, but his true passion was ministry. He was wholeheartedly committed to God's call. I caught that same fire. We didn't neglect our studies, we excelled in them, but we knew our lives were meant for something greater than grades or even personal achievement. We were called to live lives of impact, and we were ready to follow wherever that calling led.

Looking back, I see how that season laid the groundwork for everything that followed. It shaped the way I lead, the way I love, and the way I live out my faith in every area, including my career.

My career journey and personal growth are deeply rooted in the values and lessons imparted by my parents, especially my mother. Her relentless pursuit of excellence, unwavering commitment to education, and intentional focus on spiritual development shaped the foundation of who I am today. The disciplined environment she created at home, though at times intense, instilled in me a deep sense of responsibility and a lifelong thirst for knowledge. That foundation has guided me in navigating both the professional world and the complexities of personal life.

My father played an equally pivotal role. His pragmatic wisdom and his quiet but powerful belief in my potential gave me the courage to enter, and thrive, in spaces where I was often the only woman, sometimes the only Black woman, and frequently the youngest voice in the room. His confidence in me taught me not to second-guess my place at the table. He didn't just support my education, he invested in it fully, both financially and emotionally. His example of technical brilliance and quiet diligence became my blueprint for what leadership could look like.

Together, my parents created a unique ecosystem, one part entrepreneurial grit, one part academic excellence, that shaped my worldview. In our home, success wasn't optional. It was expected. But more importantly, purpose and service were not just spoken about; they were lived out daily. Their belief in me powered my journey from Nigeria to Cornell University and beyond.

My early experiences, rigid study routines, afternoons filled with reading, the balance between chores and academics, taught me to manage complexity early. And those lessons have stayed with me. They became the tools I would later use to juggle high-stakes projects in tech, raise a family, serve in ministry, and navigate leadership in multiple arenas.

As I reflect on their influence, I realize their legacy is far more than the education they provided. It's the values they instilled: discipline, integrity, resilience, and a deep sense of calling. These are the same values I now strive to pass on to my own children, because I've seen firsthand how they can shape not just careers, but entire lives.

And then there was Pastor Kay.

Meeting him as a young woman changed everything. His passion for God, his humility, and his unwavering commitment to purpose breathed new life into my faith. He helped me unlearn rigid religiosity and embrace a grace-filled relationship with God. His influence gave me the courage to pursue purpose over comfort, and to say yes to a path that didn't always make logical sense—but made divine sense.

My marriage has been more than a love story; it's been a calling. It's given me a partner who challenges, affirms, and grows with me. Together, we've navigated the tensions between faith and ambition, purpose and practicality. And through it all, I've discovered that a career rooted in conviction, guided by faith, and supported by love is not only possible but also powerful.

Ultimately, the story of my career isn't just about degrees or job titles. It's about the people who believed in me before I fully believed in myself. It's about the choices I made to live with intention. And it's about honoring the legacy of those who came before me, by living fully, giving generously, and walking confidently in the direction of purpose.

The journey from those early structured days to the purpose-driven career I now lead was no accident. It was built on intentional lessons of discipline, excellence, faith, and resilience that continue to anchor and propel me today.

Five Lessons on Consecration from Chapter 1

1. **Discipline Builds the Framework for Success**

   A consecrated life doesn't begin in the boardroom—it begins in the quiet routines of our early years. The discipline my mother instilled through structure, routine, and high expectations created the foundation for how I approach my faith and my career. Discipline, I've learned, isn't restrictive; it's liberating. It equips us to pursue excellence with focus and clarity and to show up consistently, even when the path is hard.

2. **Excellence and Faith Are Not Opposites**

   Too often, we separate spiritual growth from professional achievement, as if we must choose one or the other. But the truth is, consecration invites us to pursue both. My childhood taught me that we don't have to shrink our ambition to honor our faith. We can aim high, work hard, and still remain rooted in spiritual values. Excellence isn't a contradiction to faith—it's an expression of it.

3. **Resilience Is Part of the Calling**

   Watching my mother rebuild her dreams, again and again, taught me that a consecrated life doesn't promise ease. It promises purpose. Her resilience, through failed ventures and personal losses, modeled what it looks like to trust God through uncertainty. Consecration doesn't exempt us from hardship but prepares us to endure it gracefully and grit.

4. **Our Values Begin at Home**

   The way we lead and how we show up in the world all start with the values we're taught. My father didn't just raise a child; he raised a visionary. His belief in discipline, integrity, and hard work shaped my worldview and influenced every decision I've made since. Consecration means choosing to live by those values, even when no one is watching.

5. **Purpose Requires Surrender**

   The moment I met my husband, and the journey we've walked together reminded me that consecration isn't just about ambition but about alignment. When we surrender our plans to a greater calling, we step into something more expansive than we could have imagined. It's not always easy. It's rarely linear. But following God's purpose, especially when it defies logic, is where true fulfillment begins.

2

Coming to America

So, how does meeting a boy change the trajectory of one's career and ministry? I'll tell you.

When I met Kayode, my pastor-turned-boyfriend, he didn't have much more than a vision and an unshakable passion for God. But I believed in him. I believed in where he was going, even if neither of us could yet see how he'd get there. At the time, I had no idea that God had plans for me beyond the borders of Nigeria. Then one day, Kayode had a powerful moment during prayer. He saw a map of America, and in that moment, he knew God was calling him there.

It wasn't just a spiritual epiphany. It was a bold, seemingly impossible directive. He had no passport, no connections, and no resources to make it happen. But I remember listening to him share that story and feeling something stir within me. What if I could help? "What if I ask my dad if I can transfer to a university in the U.S.?" I offered. "What if I go first, and we figure out how you can join me later?" Of course, I wasn't planning to tell my father I was headed to America to help a boy fulfill his destiny. Deep down, I knew it would be a good move for me too; a chance to pursue a world-class education, something I had always dreamed about but hadn't fully prioritized until now.

The weekend we buried my grandmother, I decided to bring it up with my dad. Nigeria's education system was in turmoil. Strikes and student protests had caused long, unpredictable breaks in our academic calendar. My father was more open to the idea than I expected. Still, he was concerned about the stories he'd heard of young girls moving to America and losing their way. He told me to do my research: find out what tests I needed, how the application process worked, and what deadlines I'd be up against.

While I was studying for exams and preparing my applications, my father was already building bridges—reaching out to relatives, identifying schools, and mapping out logistics. After I completed my exams and submitted my paperwork, two admission offers came through. It wasn't just my preparation; it was the groundwork he had been quietly laying for months.

His support was quiet but relentless, ensuring that by the time my exams were complete, doors were already waiting to open. He reached out to relatives in the U.S. and began mapping out the logistics. I still had to write my exams, draft my essays, and prepare my applications, but he was working just as hard to make sure I had every opportunity to succeed. Looking back, I realize how much of the foundation he had laid before I even asked for help.

I remember driving with him to Obafemi Awolowo University to request my transcript. Because of the university's policies, I had to get the Dean's approval. The Dean was hesitant—he didn't want to release my records. "You're one of my best students," he said. It took some persuasion, and the gentle insistence of one of my father's friends, also a professor, to finally get the green light.

My dad then organized my documents for the U.S. embassy interview, anticipating the exact order the consular officer would ask for them. He rehearsed the conversation with me, coaching me on how to speak confidently and truthfully. Though I had only been to America once, as a toddler, my father had been many times, for both work and leisure. He understood how the system worked, and he prepared me with precision.

The visa interview went smoothly. I got my approval, packed my bags, and said my goodbyes to my siblings, friends, extended family, and, most emotionally, to Kayode. Parting ways with him was hard, harder than I expected. We didn't know when we'd see each other again. We thought maybe a year, maybe I'd visit home annually. We were wrong. It would be three years before we reunited.

Before I left, I told my mom about our relationship. I expected hesitation. After all, we came from very different backgrounds. But my mother, ever the wise and open-hearted woman, listened. I left for America soon after our conversation, trusting that she would keep an open mind. She invited Kayode over to the house to meet her, and they developed a fast bond. In the months that followed, Kayode continued to build trust with my family, visiting often, supporting them, and becoming part of their everyday lives. His consistency eventually won over even my father, although it took time and quiet persistence.

My dad, however, remained in the dark, at least at first. He often wondered why this young man was constantly around. Kayode visited regularly, built genuine relationships with each of my siblings, and stayed close to my mom. Eventually, my dad grew suspicious. "He's clearly interested in someone in this family," he thought. "But it can't be the girls, they're too young. And certainly not Mayowa. She's in America!"

When he finally learned the truth, that Kayode had remained loyal to me, stayed present for my family, and built trust in my absence, he was stunned. But more than that, he was deeply impressed. By the time my father understood the full picture, I was already thousands of miles away. This was about a year after I arrived in the US. His eventual approval, though delayed, felt like a quiet blessing over the journey I had already embarked on. It brought peace to my heart and renewed my hope, faith, and deep sense of purpose in America.

I arrived in the United States on August 13, 1995, a nineteen-year-old girl with big dreams and a heart full of purpose. I had been admitted to the University of Oklahoma to study electrical engineering, and thanks to the credits I transferred from Obafemi Awolowo University, I started as a sophomore.

Landing in America was both exhilarating and disorienting. Everything was new, unfamiliar, and fast. But it was also the beginning of something sacred; an experience that would shape not just my academic trajectory but my faith and sense of self. I focused on what mattered most: the assignment I believed God had brought me here for, and my education. With that clarity, distractions had no room to grow. I poured myself into the pursuit of excellence.

Oklahoma, in many ways, became my spiritual training ground. Ironically, I had left a thriving campus fellowship in Nigeria, where I was spiritually nourished and surrounded by people who shared my passion for God, for a quieter, more isolated setting. But that struggle, that solitude, shaped me. It taught me how to pray when no one else was praying. How to study the Word when there was no midweek service or spiritual hype. How to lean into faith when no one was watching.

It was in that quiet, often lonely space that I discovered the kind of faith that works. I listened to teachings by Kenneth Hagin, Kenneth Copeland, Creflo Dollar, and Charles Capps, and I didn't just listen; I practiced. I applied the principles they taught to my daily life, especially to my academics.

There was one semester that tested everything I was learning. I signed up for six classes. Four of them were core electrical engineering courses, and two were electives. I decided that semester would be my proving ground. "Lord," I prayed, "I'm going to apply these faith principles fully. My goal is straight A's. If it works, I'll never live any other way." It worked. I got all A's. Not just because I studied, but because I believed. That semester didn't just shape my GPA. It shaped my life philosophy.

If I could do Oklahoma all over again, I'd allow myself more room to breathe, to explore, to enjoy the experience. But if I had, I might have missed the deeper purpose. I might have missed the foundation that prepared me for ministry and for marriage.

Because yes, I stayed in that relationship with *the boy*.

It wasn't easy. We were in a long-distance relationship for nearly three years, in a world without WhatsApp, Instagram, or even consistent email access. Kayode was in Nigeria. I was in America. Communication was slow and sparse. Letters took weeks, sometimes months, to reach each other. When we could, we sent them through mutual friends or family members traveling between countries. Once in a while, we'd splurge on a quick phone call, ten minutes, max, due to the cost. We'd cram as much love and life into those few minutes as possible, then live off those words for weeks. It was love sustained by intention, built on commitment and belief, not convenience.

Those letters weren't just romantic, they were foundational. They included stories from his day-to-day life, yes, but also vision. Purpose. Ministry. Passion. Kayode shared what God was showing him about our future, about the people we were called to serve, about the work ahead. He wrote about the fellowships he was planting, the teaching meetings he was leading, the lives he was touching even while doing his national service (NYSC) and his housemanship as a pharmacy graduate. In his words, I traveled with him. I stood beside him in Abia. I helped him counsel people in a small chemist in Ibadan. I sat beside him at teaching sessions in Ife. I was there in spirit, and his letters made it real.

Every letter followed a rhythm. First, the everyday updates. Then the deep spiritual revelations. Teachings. Scriptures. Ministry plans. And finally, the romance—always tender, always intentional. His letters were like the epistles of Paul, filled with instruction, encouragement, and love. He called me his "Gem of Reality." He wrote poems for me. I fell in love with his words, and through them, with him, over and over again.

In some ways, I have a quiet pride about our love story. It wasn't built on proximity or convenience. It was built on purpose. We had no distractions, only words. And those words laid a foundation of trust, friendship, and vision that still anchors us today.

After earning my degree at the University of Oklahoma, I returned to Nigeria for two months. I thought the next step would be to find a job, ideally with a company that would sponsor my immigration status so Kayode could eventually join me. But that door didn't open. What opened instead was an opportunity to pursue my master's degree at Cornell University.

At the time, it felt like a detour. In hindsight, it was a divine redirection that worked out for my good.

I couldn't have succeeded in America without the unwavering support of family.

My journey began the day I landed in Dallas, Texas, where I was welcomed by my father's cousin, Uncle Ainde. He picked me up from the airport and became my first bridge to a new life in America.

Uncle Ainde and his brother, Uncle Isaac, worked closely together to ensure my transition to America was as smooth as possible. When I first arrived in Dallas, it was Uncle Ainde who welcomed me at the airport. He was my first bridge to a new life. Long before I boarded that plane, he had already researched schools, reviewed applications, and guided my father toward the best academic path for me. His foresight and commitment gave me the confidence I needed to begin this new chapter.

In Oklahoma, it was Uncle Isaac and his incredible wife, Aunt Alice, who became my legal guardians during my years at the University of Oklahoma. They weren't just guardians; they became my home away from home in a land that felt completely foreign. Their support was constant and generous, and years later, I would come to realize just how rare, and priceless, that kind of commitment truly is.

Over two decades of pastoring in Chicago, I've seen the other side. I've witnessed too many international students arrive in America with the promise of support, only to be cast out by relatives when the burden of hosting became inconvenient. That never happened with Uncle Isaac and Aunt Alice. Not once did they make me feel like I didn't belong. They made room for me in every sense; emotionally, logistically, spiritually. Uncle Isaac always showed up at the end of every school year in his reliable red truck, helping me move in and out of dormitories. Aunt Alice sent me warm, home-cooked meals that tasted like Nigeria and made sure I never felt the ache of homesickness at the dinner table. Whether it was Thanksgiving, Christmas, or just another weekend, I was never without family.

That consistency was transformative. Their hospitality wasn't just kindness but was also a foundation of safety and belonging in a place where I could have easily felt invisible. And it didn't stop there. Uncle Isaac's journey wasn't just about supporting me, it also became a powerful testimony in its own right.

During my time at OU, Uncle Isaac experienced a spiritual awakening that shaped both his life and mine. Fueled by a renewed relationship with God, he enrolled in a dual graduate program; psychology and counseling, paired with theological studies. It was the beginning of his own consecrated career, one that emerged not from perfect planning but from a deep desire to redeem lost time and live with purpose.

He worked hard, harder than most would dare, and after two years, he emerged with not just degrees but a new identity. He launched a counseling practice and planted a church, blending his gifts of wisdom, empathy, and faith. That church became a place of spiritual refuge for many. His counseling office became a space for healing and hope. And through it all, he remained authentic, humble, and deeply committed to serving others.

To this day, Uncle Isaac is a pillar in the community. His story reminds me that it's never too late to begin again, never too late to find your calling, and never too late to align your career with your convictions. His journey didn't just inspire me, it shaped me. He showed me what it means to lead with faith, to serve with love, and to turn your life into a testimony.

While family laid my foundation, community helped me stand. At OU, I was part of a small but deeply connected African student community. We leaned on one another. We went to church together. We formed Bible study groups. We celebrated birthdays and holidays. In a place that often felt cold and distant, we created warmth. My younger brother, the one closest to me in age, joined me a year later. Having him nearby softened the ache of homesickness. He was outgoing, and through him, I made even more friends. Having him nearby softened the ache of homesickness and gave me a renewed sense of belonging.

Accountability was another gift I didn't know I needed. I spoke often of Kayode, my long-distance boyfriend, my partner in purpose, and that openness kept me grounded. I remember a day when I was assigned to help a visiting graduate student assimilate into campus life. He was kind and intelligent, and we spent a fair amount of time together. One afternoon, as we walked and laughed our way through campus, we bumped into a friend of mine, Tokunbo. She looked at us, smiled politely, and then asked, "Kayode nko?", meaning, "How's Kayode?"

It was a simple question, but I knew what she meant. She didn't shame me or call me out. She reminded me, graciously, of what mattered. That moment was a turning point. I adjusted, created distance, and protected what I valued most. Sometimes, all it takes is one friend and one question to keep you on course.

I can't overstate the importance of the Christian community in helping us uphold our values. We all think we're strong enough to stand on our own, but we're not. We need people who remind us of who we are and what we're called to.

Another place that shaped me deeply was the African Christian Fellowship (ACF). Though registered as a campus student group, it was powered by older adults—many of them alumni and local residents—who cared about the souls of African students like me. They brought hot food from home—jollof rice, fried plantain, moinmoin—and served it with joy. Some students came just for the food. But I stayed for the community. Over time, ACF became a family. I found aunties, uncles, mentors, and prayer partners. And one of them, Mrs. Ayeni, asked me a question that changed how I saw my relationship: "Do you pray for Kayode regularly?"

That conversation marked the beginning of something beautiful. I became intentional about interceding for him—for his ministry, his leadership, and his heart. Even when we were physically apart, we were connected through prayer.

Those years were formative. They taught me that love isn't just about emotion but about alignment, that purpose isn't a destination but a daily decision, and that you can't do life alone, not the kind of life that's built to last.

Eventually, I was asked to serve as president of the fellowship—a humbling appointment, especially considering that many of the members were older than I was. But that was the beauty of the African Christian Fellowship. These men and women prioritized purpose over position, mission over hierarchy. Their shared commitment to seeing African students on campus reached with the gospel far outweighed any concern about age or status. They believed in me, and more importantly, they believed in the work we were doing together.

I led the fellowship for a semester and then handed over the baton to a graduate student who took the vision even further. Under his leadership, the student outreach continued to grow and thrive. That legacy would continue in powerful ways. Years later, my husband and I returned to OU to host revival meetings, organized by the students of ACF. Each gathering drew over a hundred students, hearts open, lives transformed. It was a full-circle moment, a reminder that seeds planted in obedience often bear fruit long after we've moved on.

ACF still exists today. Although it's no longer based directly on the OU campus, its reach has only expanded. They now support mission work around the globe and continue to hold monthly gatherings. Many of the original adult members remain actively involved, still mentoring students with the same generosity of spirit I experienced years ago. I am one of countless lives they've touched, and I carry their influence with deep gratitude.

My time at the University of Oklahoma came to a close in May of 1998. My mother flew in from Nigeria to be with me on graduation day. I'll never forget how proudly she wore her African attire, standing tall as she watched her first child cross the stage. That moment held more than academic significance; it symbolized sacrifice, vision realized, and promises fulfilled.

Kayode's letters and messages were more than love notes throughout my college years. They were reminders of the bigger picture. His words kept me anchored when distractions tempted me to go off course. They stirred my faith and reignited my focus, again and again.

Even as I poured myself into my studies, I never lost sight of the calling that had brought me to the U.S. in the first place. I wasn't just there to earn a degree. I was on assignment. That sense of purpose shaped my decisions, informed my discipline, and demanded something deeper than ambition - consecration.

Five Lessons on Consecration from Chapter 2

1. **Lead with Vision and Faith**
   Consecration often begins with a vision, one that's bigger than comfort, certainty, or immediate reward. Supporting Kayode's calling while pursuing my own education in the U.S. was a decision rooted in shared purpose. We didn't have all the answers, but we had clarity about the assignment. That kind of faith doesn't eliminate the temptation to be afraid. It simply refuses to be controlled by it. Consecration calls us to walk into the unknown, believing that what we're building is worth the sacrifice.

2. **Surround Yourself with a Supportive Circle**
   No one climbs alone. From my parents' unwavering support to the kindness of Uncle Isaac and Aunt Alice, my journey was shaped by people who believed in me and created space for me to thrive. Consecration doesn't mean doing it all yourself. It means choosing relationships that reinforce your values and sustain your momentum. It means letting others carry you when the weight of your calling feels heavy.

3. **Balance with Intention**
   Living a consecrated life is about showing up fully in every area that matters. My years in Oklahoma taught me that academic rigor and spiritual depth

weren't mutually exclusive. In fact, they fueled one another. I learned to hold my purpose close while pursuing excellence in the classroom. Consecration means being intentional about how you allocate your time and energy, so your priorities align with what you say you value.

4. **Sacrifice is Part of the Calling**
   Behind every meaningful pursuit is a willingness to let go of something else. My parents gave sacrificially so I could chase opportunities they never had. I said no to distractions so I could say yes to something greater. Consecration invites us to make hard choices not for the sake of suffering, but because we're anchored in something that matters more. It's about trading temporary comfort for lasting impact.

5. **Stay the Course—But Stay Flexible**
   Purpose doesn't always unfold in straight lines. My time at the University of Oklahoma required me to adapt constantly; academically, culturally, and emotionally. Still, I stayed rooted in the assignment. Consecration isn't about perfection or predictability. It's about commitment that bends without breaking, resolve that adjusts without giving up. When life shifts, consecration helps you stay aligned with your why, even if you have to change the how.

3

Life at Cornell

I didn't expect to get into Cornell.

I knew I was a good student, but "Ivy League" felt like a stretch. The decision to go to grad school wasn't part of a long-term plan; it was a last-minute pivot. As graduation approached at the University of Oklahoma, I hadn't landed a job, and as an international student, I needed a legal way to remain in the U.S. I was also still holding on to a vision that somehow, through me, my fiancé would find a way to come to America and fulfill the ministry assignment we both believed God had given him.

It would've been easy to quit then. I was exhausted by the distance. We had been apart for years. I missed home. I missed him. And returning to Nigeria would have meant being together again. But something in me knew I couldn't give up, not yet. Even though the pull to return home was strong, I knew my journey wasn't finished yet, not just for my career, but for the larger purpose we both believed in. Graduate school wasn't simply a way to stay in the U.S.; it was a way to keep building toward the future we had glimpsed together. So, I applied to graduate school.

I sent out three applications. The University of Oklahoma offered automatic admission to the program I was already in. Georgia Tech rejected me. And with that, I concluded my journey. If Georgia Tech said no, surely Cornell would too.

Then the letter came.

It was bulkier than a rejection usually is, but I didn't think much of it. I opened it, bracing for polite regret. Instead, I read: *"Congratulations, you have been admitted."*

I jumped. I screamed. I cried. I rolled on the floor.

And then I panicked.

There was no scholarship. No assistantship. And my parents were already carrying the financial weight of two children in college. As an international student, I couldn't legally work enough to cover both tuition and living expenses. Reality set in quickly: there was no way I could afford Cornell.

My mother, now in heaven, was a remarkable woman. She and my father had sacrificed so much for our education. She happened to be in Oklahoma early for my graduation, and when I told her the news, both the joy and the fear, she said something I'll never forget: "Don't worry. I'll talk to your dad."

They asked me how much it would cost. I told them I'd find a way to cover my living expenses through a campus job or assistantship. All they needed to think about was tuition. It was still a lot to ask. But without flinching, they agreed.

Their willingness to stretch even further, to make one more sacrifice, changed everything. That's what consecration looks like sometimes. It's not always loud. Sometimes it's the quiet decision to believe in someone else's future, even when the numbers don't add up.

Before heading to Cornell, I went back to Nigeria for two months. The reunion with Kayode was unforgettable. After nearly three years of long-distance love, letter by letter, call by call, we were finally face to face. It felt like a dream.

But what amazed me even more was how much the ministry had grown. When I left, we were a modest campus fellowship with around forty members. Now, there was a full church in Lagos. Home fellowships had sprung up. Teaching centers were thriving. It was humbling to see how God had taken those early seeds and multiplied them.

And something else had taken root in me during my time in Oklahoma: a deep interest in sound engineering. During my final year at OU, before graduation, I found myself drawn to the Media Department at Riverside Church. It started with curiosity, but under the mentorship of Paul, a seasoned sound engineer, it quickly became a passion. I immersed myself in audio production, learning the ins and outs of a discipline I'd never imagined I'd love. It was the beginning of a new skill set that would serve me for years to come.

One of the first skills I mastered in the Media Department was learning how to operate a soundboard—a maze of sliders, knobs, and buttons that, to the untrained eye, looked like an aircraft cockpit. Each control managed a specific part of the audio experience, and understanding how they worked together became my mission.

I learned how to set gain levels with precision, ensuring each microphone and instrument was heard clearly without distortion. Signal flow, how audio travels from the source through the board and out to the speakers, became second nature. I was mastering a technical language that, while invisible to the average person, was vital to every service we held.

Equalization, or EQ, became another key skill. I adjusted frequencies to shape the sound, adding richness to bass tones, softening harsh treble, and clearing up muddiness in the mids. I also learned the importance of compressors and limiters to maintain a consistent sound across instruments and voices. These tools helped prevent clipping and allowed me to create a smooth, polished mix.

During live services, I was responsible for balancing it all in real-time. The goal was simple: make sure every voice, every instrument, every moment could be heard and felt. I mixed sound for the congregation and created monitor mixes for musicians on stage, ensuring they could hear themselves and each other; a detail most people never think about, but one that deeply affects performance and worship.

Effects like reverb and delay became part of my creative toolbox. Used wisely, they added depth to the worship experience, enhancing the atmosphere without overwhelming it. I eventually began working with digital audio workstations (DAWs), recording multi-track audio from services, editing, mixing, and producing CDs and digital content. It wasn't just about making things sound good; it was about capturing moments in time and making them timeless.

When I returned to Nigeria after my degree, I didn't leave those skills behind. I brought them with me, along with a deep sense of stewardship. I conducted training sessions for local church media teams, introducing them to techniques for better microphone placement, minimizing feedback, and understanding room acoustics. In sharing what I had learned, I was helping build capacity and excellence, which mattered deeply to me.

Sound engineering had become more than a technical interest; it was a ministry in itself. My ability to serve through sound allowed the message to be heard, literally and figuratively, and it became a quiet, yet powerful, expression of my calling.

Those two months in Nigeria passed quickly, and soon it was time to return to the U.S. for graduate school. I wished Kayode and I could have gotten married then. We were so close. But the timing wasn't right. Before I left, he gave me an engagement ring. I was now officially his fiancée. Though we weren't yet at the finish line, we could finally see it.

Graduate school brought its own surprises, starting with my living arrangements.

When I arrived at Cornell, I hadn't done my homework. I hadn't researched Ithaca or looked into housing. I flew into JFK with two suitcases and asked, quite casually, how to get to Cornell. I was told to catch a Greyhound bus from LaGuardia. The six-hour ride was long, and I arrived in Ithaca with no plan. I checked into a charming bed and breakfast for the night, comforted by the warmth of a homemade breakfast the next morning. Then I began my apartment hunt.

School housing was full. The agency I referred to had only one option: a three-bedroom townhouse. There was just one complication: another person wanted the same space, and we couldn't afford it individually. The bigger twist? The other person was a man.

He was Spanish, fourteen years older, and seemed respectful and quiet. The townhouse was spacious, and we'd each have our own rooms, with a third room between us. Still, I was apprehensive. This wasn't how I imagined my Ivy League experience starting. I called my parents. I called Kayode. I laid it all out, nerves and all.

Kayode's response surprised me. He didn't hesitate. "I trust you," he said. "If this is what you have to do, then do it."

That moment reminded me of something important: trust isn't just about the absence of fear; it's about choosing faith in someone's integrity even when the circumstances aren't ideal.

While the living arrangement settled one immediate challenge, surviving day-to-day as a graduate student brought its own set of battles, most of them financial

My master's program at Cornell was a nine-month sprint, a professional M.Eng. degree in Electrical Engineering. I had promised my parents I would cover my living expenses so they could focus solely on tuition. It was a well-meaning commitment, but one that left me struggling through the year more than I anticipated. Looking back, I should have told them how hard it really was. They would have helped me. When I eventually shared with my mother how often I had gone hungry in New York, she was devastated. "How could my daughter have been starving herself while I ate freely at home?" she asked through tears.

The reality was that I went hungry more days than I care to remember. I developed persistent headaches from the lack of food. I fell behind on rent. My housemate, an older man, was patient with me, until he wasn't. One day, after I had missed a few too many payments, he finally spoke up. "And don't think I haven't noticed you've been taking my bananas," he said bluntly. He wasn't wrong. I had quietly taken a few without asking, hoping he wouldn't notice. It was humbling. He never crossed any lines; we respected each other's space, and nothing inappropriate ever happened. But it's not a story I tell often, because not everyone can understand the complexities or the quiet desperation of that season. I wouldn't recommend the arrangement to anyone. It wasn't ideal. But I'm thankful for the trust of my fiancé, who supported me from afar with grace and understanding.

One of the things that anchored me during that season was giving. Even when I barely had enough, I continued to sow financial seeds into ministries that had fed me spiritually. Each month, I gave, even if it was small, and I spoke over my seed: "This ministry may not know me, but the anointing on their life recognizes me. That anointing is working on my life, my future, my ministry, and my marriage." It wasn't just an act of faith but my way of declaring that my circumstances did not define me.

Ithaca was both a challenge and a gift. It became a sacred season of training.

I had grown spiritually in Oklahoma, but in Ithaca, I learned to walk with the Holy Spirit on a deeper level. I spoke to Him on my walks to class, in the quiet of my room, in the solitude that only a place like Cornell, tucked in the hills of upstate New York, could provide. Ezra Cornell once said, "I would found an institution where anyone can find instruction in any field of study." When asked how he would do that, he replied, "Just wait until you see where I put it." He wasn't wrong. Ithaca was remote, but that remoteness gave me focus.

I decided to start a small Christian fellowship at Cornell. I had missed the opportunity to lead one during my undergrad years, and I didn't want to miss it again. We met on Fridays. We never grew beyond five people, but I pastored that tiny group with all my heart. I shared everything I was learning from Kenneth Hagin and from my fiancé and pastor, Kayode Ijisesan. On Saturdays, we would gather at a local café and study the Bible for hours. Our small group once collaborated with larger African and Singaporean fellowships to host a worship event that drew students from across campus. It was beautiful.

That connection with the Singaporean fellowship continued. I was invited to teach their Bible studies, and often those sessions ended with the prophetic. Years later, when I visited Singapore, members of that same group gathered for dinner and shared how the prophecies from those meetings had come to pass. I was stunned, and grateful that God had used the young woman I was back then to make such an impact.

One person who played a pivotal role during my time at Cornell was Professor Alfred Phillips. He was assigned as my mentor, and though he was in his sixties, he had the energy of someone half his age, still running marathons and mentoring students with infectious enthusiasm. He offered me a graduate assistantship, which helped immensely with finances. For my final project, I proposed something called IBNet, which was an idea to bring internet access to Ibadan, Nigeria, using a mix of satellite and wired technology. Communication with my parents and Kayode had been so difficult that the concept felt urgent and personal. Professor Phillips believed in the idea and encouraged me to pursue it. IBNet served as my capstone project at Cornell, successfully completed for graduation, but it never moved beyond the academic stage. I wish now that I had taken it further. At a place like Cornell, where innovation thrives, I might have been at the forefront of a solution that was desperately needed. But I was focused on survival and finishing my degree. Sometimes I wonder what could've been if I had allowed myself to dream a little bigger in that moment.

Academically, Cornell pushed me hard. My coursework in software-focused electrical engineering was intense and fast-paced. There were times I feared I would fail, but I finished strong, mostly A's, a few B's. Still, the pressure left a mark. Even now, I sometimes wake from dreams where I've missed exams or failed to graduate. In those dreams, I carry the weight of disappointing my parents and wasting their sacrifices. I always wake up relieved that it was only a dream, but those moments remind me how deeply that season shaped me.

Determined not to repeat my post-graduation scramble from undergrad, I started my job search early. I worked closely with the Career and Academic Counseling Department, polished my résumé, practiced interview skills, and took every opportunity seriously. It paid off. I received an offer from Altera, a tech company in San Jose. The base salary was $65,000, an enormous sum in 1999, and more than I ever expected. At first, I hesitated. I felt pulled in another direction spiritually, but wise counsel helped me discern that this was an open door I should walk through. I accepted the offer, and my new employer covered my relocation costs, including my flight and first month's accommodation.

With graduation complete and my job offer secured, I had a week before my start date, a perfect window to attend a Christian conference in Los Angeles, something I had long looked forward to. I had one request. I wanted to be at that Christian conference. They agreed to route my flight through LA. I was excited, but financially, I was at my limit. I left Ithaca with just $50 to my name.

By the first night of the conference, I had just $23 left. My accommodation was covered, but food for the week? That was a problem. During the offering that evening, I made a decision: I wasn't going to stretch that money across a few meals. I was going to stretch my faith. I gave the entire $23 in the offering and committed to a fast for the rest of the week. Day three was the toughest. I felt lightheaded, but I pushed through.

During the conference, I met a man from San Francisco, a manager at Oracle, newly saved, originally from Taiwan. We bonded over our shared love of tech and faith. We talked during breaks, swapped notes on sessions, and grew a fast friendship. Each day, he invited me to lunch. Each day, I politely declined. I never told him I was fasting. I never told him I didn't have the money to eat.

By the third day of the fast, I was light-headed and felt I couldn't go on. That was the hardest day, though, as things got easier after that. On the last day of the conference, as we said our goodbyes, my new friend shook my hand and slipped something into my palm. "God told me to give this to you," he said. It felt like an envelope. I assumed it was a small cash gift, maybe $20 or $50. But when I opened it, my breath caught. It was a check for $1,000.

It was more than a financial gift. It was a reminder: God saw me. He had seen the $23 I dropped in the offering plate. He had seen my sacrifice. He had seen me walk through that week without asking anyone for help. And He had moved the heart of someone I barely knew to meet a need I had never voiced.

That check carried me through my first few days in San Jose. I used it to open my first bank account. It kept me going until my first paycheck. And with it, a new chapter began - my journey in Silicon Valley.

Looking back, the path from the University of Oklahoma to Cornell to San Jose was anything but smooth. But it was full of growth. It tested my resilience, deepened my faith, and taught me to trust God in ways I never imagined. Every sacrifice, every detour, every fast, and every tear was preparing me for something bigger than myself.

Five Lessons on Consecration from Chapter 3

1. **Trusting God as Provider**

    My journey to Cornell was filled with uncertainty, especially financially. But I learned that consecration isn't just about spiritual devotion; it's about surrendering practical needs to God's provision. Even when I doubted, God made a way through people, opportunities, and moments I never could have predicted. Consecration means choosing trust over control, even when the numbers don't add up.

2. **Staying Committed to Purpose**

    There were plenty of reasons to give up, including fatigue from long-distance love, the pressure of staying in the U.S., and the sheer weight of uncertainty. But I stayed rooted in the vision God had given us. Consecration demands that we hold fast to divine purpose even when it's uncomfortable, inconvenient, or unclear. Purpose isn't always easy, but it's always worth it.

3. **Giving When It Hurts**

   In the middle of financial struggle, I chose to give, sowing into ministries that fed me spiritually. It wasn't about the amount; it was about the posture of my heart. Consecration is marked by generosity, not just when it's easy, but when it stretches us. It's trusting that when we give God our best, especially when it costs us, He responds with abundance.

4. **Growing in the Quiet**

   Ithaca was quiet. Isolated. Sometimes lonely. But that stillness became sacred. In solitude, I developed a deeper sensitivity to the Holy Spirit. I learned to walk with God more personally, more intimately. Consecration isn't forged in the spotlight. It's refined in the quiet, where our roots grow deep and our trust grows stronger.

5. **Enduring with Grace**

   Nothing about that season was easy. From delayed rent to academic pressure and cultural shifts, it demanded grit. But I kept going. Consecration requires perseverance; the ability to keep showing up, keep believing, and keep pressing forward. Even when the journey is uphill, we trust that God is shaping something greater than we can see.

4

Silicon Valley

The first time I walked into Altera's offices as a new hire, I felt a heady mix of excitement and apprehension. I was stepping into the heart of Silicon Valley, one of the world's most dynamic centers of technological innovation. And I was finally here, not as a visitor, but as a contributing engineer. I had interviewed on-site before, but this time was different. This time, I had a badge. I belonged.

At least, that's what I told myself.

Altera embodied much of what the Valley stood for: cutting-edge thinking, world-class talent, and a relentless drive to build the future. Teams were international, multidisciplinary, and deeply committed to pushing the boundaries of programmable logic. There was an undeniable buzz in the air. You could feel it in the sleek glass architecture, the hum of collaboration, and the pace at which ideas moved. It was thrilling to be part of something so forward-looking.

But as the buzz settled and I found my rhythm, something quieter but equally present emerged: the realization that I was an outlier. And not just professionally.

I was one of the few women in my department, and the only Black person, not just in my team, but in the entire Software Engineering division and most professional departments around me.

This wasn't a shock. I had grown used to being "the only one" in many classrooms and project teams back in college. Still, somewhere deep down, I had hoped the professional world might look different. I thought that maybe, just maybe, I'd walk into a room and see more people who looked like me. But here I was again.

The truth is, companies are fed by the pipeline of colleges and universities. And if there aren't enough women or people of color in tech programs, there won't be enough in tech companies. The numbers don't lie. And they don't shift without intentional effort.

What I hadn't anticipated was how much that invisibility would weigh on me. Being a minority often means carrying an unspoken, additional burden—the burden of proving that you belong, that you're not just a hire to check a box, that your voice deserves a place at the table. That burden can be isolating.

I remember team-wide meetings where more than 150 engineers gathered together. Inevitably, the seats to my left and right would be the last ones filled. I don't believe anyone intentionally avoided sitting next to me. People simply gravitate toward what's familiar. And at the time, there wasn't as much awareness or dialogue around race, inclusion, or the lived experience of being "the only one." My colleagues were smart, capable, even warm, but they didn't see my isolation. Not because they were unkind. But because they didn't know how much it cost to keep showing up feeling unseen.

I was also an introvert, and that didn't help. I didn't initiate conversations easily. I waited, hoping someone would notice me, include me, pull me into their circle. Sometimes they did. Many times, they didn't.

Pastoring has shaped me over the years. I've learned to lead with warmth and initiate with confidence. But back then, I was still waiting to be invited in. And more often than not, I was met with silence.

These early days at Altera taught me an important lesson: inclusion isn't just about who's in the room, it's about who feels welcome once they get there.

And belonging isn't a given. Sometimes, it's something we have to build for ourselves and for those coming after us.

Despite the challenges of being one of the only women, and the only Black woman, in my department, I threw myself into the work. I loved what I was doing. I was working on layouts for programmable control boards (PCBs) used to test our devices, and I also performed device testing in the lab. The hands-on experience was exhilarating. I soldered components for the first time; a skill

I never imagined would be part of my career, and thanks to patient guidance from my boss, Nick Rally, and my colleague Jean Nicole-Pierre, I quickly got the hang of it.

What made the work even more meaningful was how critical it was to the business. Jean designed the boards, and I managed the layout and manufacturing process. Every decision I made had weight, real consequences. A small mistake in the layout could render an entire board useless, costing the company thousands of dollars. There was no room for "close enough."

I'll never forget the first time I submitted a board layout to Nick. I handed it to him and, when he asked if everything was correct, I said something like, "I did my best." He looked at me and said, "Go do it again." At the time, I didn't understand why he was being so particular. But I soon realized that in engineering, especially in high-stakes environments like this one, good intentions aren't enough. Precision is non-negotiable. That lesson stuck with me. It taught me the importance of obsessing over details, of checking and rechecking your work. "Good enough" simply wasn't good enough. It had to be right.

In addition to my work on hardware, I was writing software too, code that interfaced directly with the programmable logic devices. This wasn't like coding in school, where the stakes were low and projects were hypothetical. This was different. This was real. My work didn't just exist on a screen, it affected products, timelines, and people. I programmed primarily in C++, drawing heavily on the object-oriented programming principles I had learned in school. But now, those principles weren't just academic, they were practical tools that helped me create solutions with real-world impact. That made my work feel more alive. And more rewarding.

Still, I made my share of mistakes. One, in particular, left a lasting impression.

One Friday, after submitting a board layout to the manufacturer, I was settling in for the weekend when a sense of panic washed over me. Something was wrong. I didn't know how I knew it, but my mind, always scanning in the background, had found a flaw. I sat up in bed, heart racing. I had flipped the main chip on the board. It was positioned on the wrong side—an error that would make the board completely unusable.

There was nothing I could do that weekend. The office was closed. So was the manufacturing site. I barely slept. I knew what the mistake meant: $15,000 in wasted materials and labor. By Monday morning, I was a wreck. But I knew I had to face it.

I walked up to Nick's cubicle and quietly explained what had happened. Together, we went to his boss and delivered the news. I expected frustration or disappointment. But what I received instead was grace. They were kind. They understood. Looking back, I realize that both of them had once been in my shoes. They had made mistakes too. And they knew that sometimes the best lessons are the most expensive ones.

That experience changed me. It reminded me that failure isn't the end of the road, it's part of the journey. It also reminded me how much leadership matters. The way leaders respond to failure can either build or break someone's confidence. That day, my leaders chose to build. And I've never forgotten that.

Another aspect of my job involved testing our chips, sometimes in ways that pushed them to their limits. While the Quality Assurance and Testing Department handled most standard evaluations, my role was to think like the end users who broke the rules, the ones who didn't read manuals, the ones who wired things just a little differently. My job was to test for the unlikely, the unusual, the extreme, and make sure our chips could still perform under those conditions.

Right before a major product launch, I was in the lab doing one of these tests, running through fringe scenarios with our latest chip and accompanying software. I was referencing a section of code written by one of my colleagues when suddenly, I smelled something faint but concerning. Burning. At first, it was barely noticeable. But a few seconds later, it was unmistakable. Something was overheating, and fast.

I paused. We were two days away from launch. The logical part of me considered letting it go. What I had just tested was so unlikely to happen in the field. Most users would never write the kind of code I had just run. But then I thought bigger. Our chips didn't just sit in labs. They powered consumer electronics. They were embedded in devices that landed in homes, offices, and even airplanes. What if someone did try this configuration? What if the failure happened out in the world, and we had ignored the warning signs?

I knew what I had to do.

I went straight to my boss and told him what I'd found. He followed me to the lab, repeated the test, and we saw the same issue. The chip allowed too much current to flow through, triggered by a specific but possible scenario. It could've been catastrophic. Our manager made the call to comment out that portion of the code, making it inactive so the product could still launch safely.

That day taught me an invaluable lesson: what we do at work matters, even the edge cases. Even the things no one else thinks are worth looking into. It's easy to get comfortable and assume someone else will catch the bugs. But responsibility in engineering means caring enough to speak up, even when it's inconvenient. Attention to detail isn't just about quality, it's about safety, integrity, and sometimes, saving people you may never meet from the consequences of silence.

I'm glad I caught that bug.

Beyond the lab, Silicon Valley was pulsing with energy and money. There was a buzz in the air, a mix of innovation and ambition that made the entire region feel like a different world. Competition between peers was subtle, but real. Every promotion, every product breakthrough, every new feature had weight. Success was visible, and so was failure.

Tech companies weren't just generous with salaries, they offered stock bonuses and options that could double, even triple your annual income if your company performed well. It became addictive to log into your investment portal and see your worth climb as quarterly earnings beat expectations. Those numbers weren't just abstract, they translated into real life. A new car. A down payment on a house. Travel. Freedom. Living in the Bay Area wasn't cheap, but if you were in tech, you were insulated from much of that pressure, at least for a while.

But this constant rush, this access to seemingly unlimited resources, also created an illusion. It was easy to think it would last forever, that the good times would keep rolling. And so when the tech bubble burst in the early 2000s, the impact hit hard. The higher the climb, the greater the fall.

It was a reality check for Silicon Valley. And for me, a reminder that careers, like markets, have cycles. There are seasons of plenty and seasons that demand grit. But regardless of the circumstances, our integrity, our work ethic, and our willingness to do the right thing, even when it's hard, are what sustain us.

My initial offer letter from Altera came with a competitive salary, but what truly caught my eye were the stock options. They wouldn't vest for another 18 months, but even before they did, I had a lot to be hopeful about. Every time the company performed well, my portfolio grew alongside it. At the end of each year, we received stock bonuses tied to company performance. This wasn't just compensation but also participation. It was investment. It gave employees a real sense of ownership, and it created momentum.

Those blessings made it easier when God instructed Kayode not to seek a job in pharmacy, but to wait. It was an unconventional choice, especially in Silicon Valley, where dual-income households were the norm. But because of the stability my job offered, we could obey. We were comfortable, and I learned early on not to measure our comfort by comparing it to what my colleagues were doing or driving. I didn't need to compete, I needed to stay aligned with purpose.

From June 1999 to August 2002, Silicon Valley was both a cradle of innovation and a storm of uncertainty. The dot-com bubble had been inflating throughout the late '90s, and in March 2000, it burst spectacularly. Once-celebrated companies with billion-dollar valuations folded overnight. Webvan. Pets.com. Each became a cautionary tale about scaling too fast on shaky ground.

But not every story was a cautionary tale. Some companies survived and came out stronger. Google, still in its early days, was quietly revolutionizing search. Apple, under Steve Jobs, was making a bold comeback with the iMac and the iPod. Amidst the noise, these companies focused on user experience, long-term vision, and innovation that mattered. They weren't chasing hype but building legacies.

Altera navigated this turbulence with a clear focus on core technology. We weren't trying to be the flashiest, we were committed to being the most dependable. That season in Silicon Valley taught me more than just business acumen. It taught me the value of vision, resilience, and staying grounded in what works, even when the world is spinning fast around you.

Outside of work, I found an unexpected gift: community. Through a connection from Oklahoma, I met a network of Nigerian Christian women in the Bay Area. They became my lifeline, both before and after Kayode joined me in California. One of the women who impacted me most was Sister Gloria—a woman of grace, grit, and unshakable faith.

She had come from Nigeria, a lawyer who had left her career to raise her family and support her husband's ministry. But life turned upside down when her husband suddenly passed away while jogging. She was pregnant with their third child and unemployed. With no time to grieve, she had to rebuild from the ground up, starting as a paralegal, slowly climbing her way back into law.

When I met her, she was a single mother doing everything she could to provide for her children while keeping them in a Christian school. She worked hard, believed fiercely, and gave freely, even when she didn't have much. Despite all she carried, she always had a smile and an open door. We carpooled to work together and had deep, meaningful conversations. As a newlywed, I absorbed so much wisdom from those car rides. Sister Gloria is one of those people who step into your life and never leave. She inspired me then, and she still does today.

Silicon Valley was also where our marriage began.

After nearly five years of a long-distance relationship, navigating multiple time zones, handwritten letters, expensive phone calls, and growing ministries, Kayode and I were finally ready. We got married on March 27, 1999, right in the middle of my last spring break at Cornell. It wasn't ideal timing, but it was divinely orchestrated.

Altera had extended their job offer to me early by October 1998, they had not only offered me a position but also promised to sponsor my H-1B visa. It was more than generous; they were even willing to file an H-4 visa for my spouse if I was married before starting. But there was one catch: the job was in California. For some reason, I believed New England was where I was supposed to be. I delayed accepting the offer, waiting for something else.

That's when Reverend Victor Adeyemi, our pastor and mentor, entered the picture.

He was visiting the U.S. and holding meetings in New York City. I traveled six hours to attend. After the meeting, we spoke. I told him about the job offer and my plan to turn it down because it wasn't in the right region. I'll never forget his reaction. "What if this is the door God has opened? And what if you got married before you started?" The idea felt wild. I was only 22. Spring break was months away. How would we plan a wedding in Nigeria in that short window?

But sometimes, when wise counsel aligns with divine timing, you say yes.

My father was planning a visit to Ithaca in October. He flew into New York and took a bus to campus. I borrowed a friend's car, picked him up, and checked him into a local hotel. We soaked up every moment of his short visit; campus tours, a road trip to see Niagara Falls, a dinner with friends, and my professor, Dr. Phillips. He even bought a Cornell T-shirt that read, "My daughter and my money go to Cornell." I still smile thinking about him wearing that around Ibadan.

At some point during the visit, I knew I had to have the hard conversation. I shared the job offer and the opportunity it presented if I was married before my start date. I was bracing for resistance. Instead, he surprised me. He had grown fond of Kayode. He admired our maturity, our patience, and the intentionality of our relationship. He understood the immigration implications and knew that saying no now could make things harder later.

He spoke with my mom. They gave their blessing. They met with Kayode's family. The introduction took place, and the wedding date was set for my spring break.

In just four months, my parents planned a beautiful wedding in Nigeria with over 1,000 guests. It was a whirlwind, but it was perfect.

Have you ever tried getting married over spring break… in another country? It's as hectic as it sounds. I flew into Lagos with my wedding dress and accessories, gifts from family members who believed in my future as much as I did. The week was a blur of ceremonies, family gatherings, and sacred moments. We managed to squeeze in a short honeymoon, and just like that, I was back on a plane to finish my degree.

It was fast. It was bold. And it was right. Sometimes consecration looks like saying yes to the unpredictable, the inconvenient, and the unconventional because purpose doesn't always wait for perfect timing.

Kayode joined me seven months later. Those were seven long months to wait. They seemed to drag on even more than the four years before. However, the day that seemed like it would never come finally arrived. On November 19, 1999, we stood in the manifestation of what we had trusted God for since I left Nigeria in August 1995. My husband joined me in California, and we started our lives together as a married couple.

God had told my husband not to start a church in California. This was a strange instruction since he had planted two churches in Nigeria by then, but we obeyed. Instead, we had monthly outreach meetings, a great way to connect with and minister to people. We took a few people through discipleship this way. It was also our first time doing ministry together after so many years. In 2000, we started bi-annual outreach meetings at my alma mater, the University of Oklahoma. The meetings had the blessing of God on them. They brought revival to the hearts and lives of many students. Hundreds of students would attend, and we saw lives transformed. It was a blessing to be able to do this together. When I attended OU, I had never imagined God would bring me back to do something like that for Him. We were blessed.

In June 2002, God told us to leave California and move to Chicago to start a church. We had received our Green Cards in record time. I was very appreciative of Altera for this. The lawyers who worked on my application were stellar, and the company made the entire process seamless.

I was ecstatic at the thought of a new adventure. My job was excellent and financially rewarding, but I would have to quit and move to Chicago with my husband. I turned in my resignation letter the same day I got a significant raise, the second one in six months. My boss called me into a conference room and wrote me a letter informing me that my salary had increased. I gave him a letter letting him know I was leaving the company. I hadn't planned that I would be informing him on the day he would be giving me a raise; it was a coincidence. He asked me if I had gotten a job in Chicago. I told him no, I wasn't moving for a job. "Why, then, are you moving?" "I am moving with my husband to start a church." He was bewildered. I saw the concern on his face, but he could not deny the excitement he saw on mine. I appreciated his genuine concern, though. Who in their right mind would leave a great job like mine to start a church in another state?

My department was very gracious to hold a send-off for me. During that sendoff, Alan Hermann, the head of the department who had also conducted my on-site interview before I was hired, said he was glad that he had taken a chance on me. He said I had brought so much value to the department, and he was thankful that he had hired me. Those words stayed with me and were a great boost to my morale as I looked forward to my next adventure.

On August 9, 2002, I arrived at Midway Airport in Chicago, nine weeks pregnant with my son, ready for what God had for us in our new city.

Five Lessons on Consecration from Chapter 4

1. **Resilience in the Face of Isolation**
   Walking into rooms where no one looks like you, or even chooses to sit beside you, can make you question your belonging. But consecration doesn't crumble under pressure; it quietly builds strength in the shadows. My early days at Altera were a masterclass in perseverance. I learned to keep showing up, keep delivering, and keep believing, even when I felt unseen. Resilience became an act of devotion: to my calling, my purpose, and the future I wanted to help build.

2. **Excellence as an Act of Faithfulness**
   There's a kind of consecration that happens when we treat our work like it matters because it does. Laying out circuit boards taught me that "good enough" isn't always good enough. A small mistake could cost thousands of dollars, or compromise a product used in homes, hospitals, or planes. Consecration, in this context, meant honoring the details. It was a daily decision to show up with precision and care, because excellence is a form of worship when it's done with the right heart.

3. **Integrity When It's Hard**
   Owning a $15,000 mistake is not for the faint of heart. But that moment, walking into my boss's cubicle, telling the truth, accepting responsibility, wasn't just about professionalism. It was about consecration. It was about doing the right thing, even when it's uncomfortable. Consecration calls us

to honesty, to humility, and to the kind of leadership that builds trust in the quiet, difficult moments, not just the celebrated ones.

4. **Adaptability in Seasons of Change**

   Between 1999 and 2002, Silicon Valley was riding a rollercoaster of innovation and instability. Some companies folded. Others emerged stronger. I learned that consecration doesn't mean avoiding turbulence, it means remaining anchored through it. It means pivoting when necessary, letting go of what no longer serves your purpose, and continuing to lead with clarity even when the ground shifts beneath your feet.

5. **The Power of Community in a Consecrated Life**

   No one fulfills their calling alone. My community, especially women like Sister Gloria, reminded me that consecration isn't just about discipline and calling. It's also about connection. It's about surrounding yourself with people who speak faith into your weary days and remind you of what's possible when everything feels uncertain. Consecration is strengthened in community. It's sustained through shared wisdom, grace, and love.

5

Marriage, Miracles, and Trying Times

When I moved to Chicago, I was nine weeks pregnant and brimming with optimism. I fully expected to land a job within weeks. I had a plan that made perfect sense to me, and I believed it made sense to God too. I would find a great new role before my pregnancy became visible, easing the financial pressure on our young family. I'd be able to show my former boss that leaving California hadn't been reckless, it had been led. Purposeful. Right.

That's not how it happened.

What happened instead were seven long months of waiting. Seven months without a job offer. Seven months of watching my confidence stretch thin while my belly grew round.

I had exactly one job interview before my son was born. It was just two weeks before my due date. Determined to hide my pregnancy, I wore a massive winter coat, one of those Chicago-worthy coats that swallows you whole. I never took it off. We were indoors, but I stayed zipped up the entire time, as if trying to convince both the interviewer and myself that everything was normal.

In hindsight, I realize how absurd that must have looked. I was visibly pregnant, coat or no coat. My face alone gave it away. I'm not saying that's why I didn't get the job. There could have been a dozen reasons. But the experience left me rattled. I had done everything I could to shape the narrative, and still, it hadn't worked.

Our son was born in March 2003. And just weeks later, I was back at it, ready to hit "Apply" again and again. But this time, I had a newborn in my arms. I was navigating midnight feedings, diaper changes, and the constant, beautiful chaos of new motherhood.

At first, I was overwhelmed. How do you job hunt with a baby? I turned to Mary Kay Ash's *Miracles Happen*, a book filled with structure, drive, and conviction. It inspired me to put some order to my day. I created a schedule: morning feedings and baths, followed by a few hours of quiet play for my son. During those windows, I sat at my computer, scouring job boards and submitting applications. Then came naptime and more job hunting.

The pressure was mounting. I was desperate. At one point, I told my husband I was considering selling knives door to door. He wasn't thrilled. But I needed to do something. I ended up joining Mary Kay as a consultant. I wasn't particularly successful in sales, but I gained something even better: community. I met extraordinary women, including my mentor and hers, and for the first time, I learned how to properly apply makeup. It may sound trivial, but it was empowering, another way I was growing into myself, one layer at a time.

Meanwhile, I threw myself into the life of our church plant. We were still in the earliest days, running operations from the basement of our rented condo. We had a wonderful woman handling the church's bookkeeping, but she worked full-time and couldn't always finish the tasks. I began stepping in to help, especially with monthly reconciliations. One day, she came in excited. She'd just taken a training at work on Microsoft Access, and she thought it could transform how we managed our church finances.

As she showed me how she was entering our records, I watched carefully. When she had to leave, I offered to keep going. I took over from where she stopped. I wanted to understand the tool, and more than that, I wanted to be useful. My background in programming helped me build on what she had started, and before long, I'd developed a basic system that handled our church's accounting needs. It wasn't fancy, but it worked. It worked for us then and for years to come.

I was genuinely excited about the opportunity. It wasn't glamorous, and it wasn't permanent, but it was something. A six-week contract role came through, and even though the pay was nowhere near what I had earned in California, it was a start. My first real job in Chicago. I was grateful.

I lined up childcare for my son, picked up a few new work clothes, and prepared myself to show up fully. The role was with a team working on decommissioning a Pfizer plant in Skokie. People from different agencies were involved, and I reported to a man from the company leading the entire project. My position? Data entry.

The old me might have bristled at that. A software engineer doing data entry? But motherhood and ministry had taught me something about humility and perspective. I didn't see the job as beneath me. I saw it as a way forward.

So I rolled up my sleeves and got to work. I completed the tasks ahead of schedule and immediately asked for more. My boss, the man I reported to, noticed. He started giving me additional, more technical assignments. I wasn't surprised. I knew what I could do.

Before long, I negotiated a small pay bump with my agency. It wasn't huge, but it meant something. It meant I was being seen.

And when I still had extra time after completing even those more complex tasks, I asked for more again. Eventually, he began handing me pieces of his job. Then, casually, he mentioned that he was talking to his boss about transitioning off the project, and when that happened, I would take over his role. "You'll get my rate," he said. Then he told me what that rate was.

I was floored.

The number stuck in my head like a song I couldn't stop playing. I imagined myself finally earning what I was worth. It gave me renewed energy. I took over his job in all but title. I managed processes, answered questions, and kept the project moving.

The initial six-week assignment had now extended to three months, and with every passing day, I kept telling myself: this is how it happens. This is how doors open.

But toward the end of the project, something started to feel off. I asked him again what was happening with the role. "Don't worry," he said. "It's in motion." I wanted to believe him. I *needed* to believe him. I reminded myself how good the title would look on my resume. I silenced my doubts.

Until I couldn't.

It hit me, suddenly and completely. I had been used.

He had no intention of advocating for me. There was no promotion coming. No new title. No increased pay. I had been doing his job while he sat in the parking lot, chewing tobacco and talking on the phone. And now, the project was ending.

I excused myself and went to the bathroom. I cried. Not polite, restrained tears. I wept. The building was nearly empty, so I had privacy. And I needed it. Because what I was crying about wasn't just that moment—it was everything leading up to it.

I cried for the move from California, full of faith and hope, only to feel like every door was closing. I cried for the countless applications, the silence, the rejections. I cried for the version of me who kept showing up, kept trying, kept believing, and kept getting pushed aside.

And I cried for how foolish I felt. How naïve. I had no paper trail. No email. Nothing to point to, nothing I could use to hold him accountable. And even if I did, I didn't have the energy to pursue it. I was done.

And then, just as clearly as the silence that had surrounded me, God spoke.

"Now wipe your eyes, return to your desk, and begin writing. I will show you some things about believers in the workplace."

So I did.

I walked back to my desk. I didn't look at him. I didn't need to. I had work to do, not for the company, but for a purpose I hadn't yet fully seen.

That day marked the beginning of something new. It was the first step toward writing my book, *Wisdom for the Workplace*. It was also the start of something even bigger, *Career Resources: Heavenly Resources for the Workplace*, an outreach I would later lead to empower believers to thrive in their careers with excellence, integrity, and purpose.

What felt like the end turned out to be a beginning. And as painful as it was, I wouldn't trade that bathroom floor moment for anything.

Because sometimes, when we feel most unseen, God is preparing us to be vessels for something greater.

That project ended, and I was back to job hunting.

What I had expected to be a short transitional period had now stretched into something longer, heavier. I thought finding a job would be quick.

Logical, even. I had experience. I had skills. I was in a new city but armed with credentials and a strong work ethic. Surely, this wouldn't take long.

But it did.

The waiting season wore me down. I cried. I complained. I spiraled. Some days, I felt deeply discouraged. Other days, I just felt trapped between my desire to move forward and the frustrating silence from employers. I took it personally. I questioned everything. Had I left too soon? Should I have stayed in California longer? And in my most vulnerable moments, I let guilt and anxiety creep into my relationship with my husband. I knew that my not working put pressure on our finances, and that added weight made every unanswered email and rejection feel like a failure, not just professionally, but personally.

Even so, I knew I had made the right decision to leave Altera and move to Chicago. Some choices are right even when the path that follows is anything but easy. Still, I hadn't realized just how difficult this chapter would be.

And then came the Receiver Corporation.

If ever there was a red flag wrapped in corporate jargon, it was this company. But hindsight, of course, always has 20/20 vision.

I got an email saying they'd seen my resume and wanted to interview me. Finally, there was movement. I hadn't had an interview in months, so this felt like a breakthrough. I squeezed money out of our tight budget and bought a new blue suit. My husband drove me to the interview. We were both hopeful. He wanted to be part of what we thought might be a turning point.

The office was in a sleek building near O'Hare. Multiple businesses shared the floors, and The Receiver Corporation had a corner on the seventh. When I walked into the waiting area, I saw about seven other people waiting to be interviewed. My first thought was: Wow, this company must be scaling. Growth like that had to be a good sign, right?

While I waited, I started chatting with another candidate. We had different professional backgrounds, but that didn't faze me right away. I just assumed this company had multiple roles to fill.

The interview was brief; fifteen minutes. Polite. Vague. I was told I had great experience, but that the job required specialized software training. Once I learned the software, I'd be eligible to start work and receive assignments. The catch? The software cost $500.

I wasn't prepared for that, but I was hungry for the opportunity. I wanted it to work. They told me I could pay right away and collect the training materials or return with a check later that day. I chose the latter.

As I left the building, I passed by even more people waiting to be interviewed. It struck me as odd, but I reasoned it away again. "Maybe they're just really growing," I told myself.

Later that day, my husband and I drove back to drop off the check. Again, new faces in the lobby. A revolving door of hopefuls.

I brought the materials home and started to study. The software was underwhelming. A clunky, Excel-based tool that felt more like a bad college project than enterprise software. The manual? Confusing at best. But I pushed through. I wanted to believe this would lead to something.

A few days later, the friend I had made at the interview called. He was struggling with the material and asked if we could meet up to work through it together. We met after church that Sunday. As we spoke, I grew more puzzled. His background wasn't remotely aligned with the kind of work I thought we were both pursuing. He didn't have a tech background or any experience in IT. It didn't make sense. How were we being hired for the same job?

Still, I tamped down my doubts. I didn't want to be cynical. I wanted this to be real.

We didn't make much progress that day. And slowly, the truth started to settle in; this wasn't what it seemed.

Eventually, I picked up the phone and called the number I'd been given to contact the company. No answer. I tried at different times of the day, hoping it was just bad timing. Still nothing. I followed up with emails. Silence.

But I kept making excuses for them. Maybe they were still conducting interviews. Maybe they were reviewing our submissions. After all, they had said to reach out in three weeks. So I waited, clinging to the possibility that this might still turn out okay.

When the three weeks were up, I drove back to the corporate building near O'Hare. I took the elevator to the seventh floor, the same one where I had sat, full of hope, just a few weeks earlier.

But the moment the elevator doors opened, I knew. The space was completely empty. No desks. No signage. No people. Just silence.

It was gone.

Everything had been cleared out. The Receiver Corporation no longer existed—not there, not anywhere. They had vanished - just like that.

I stood there in shock. And then, like a spreadsheet flipping through my mind, I started to do the math.

Seven interviewees per hour. Eight hours a day. Five days a week. For three weeks.

Assuming just half of them paid the $500 for the so-called training software, and that's a conservative estimate, that would've been $210,000. Subtract the cost of the short-term office rental and some miscellaneous expenses, and they'd likely walked away with at least $190,000.

In 2003, that was a fortune.

And every single dollar had come from people like me; people desperate for a fresh start, people clinging to hope, people willing to believe in an opportunity because the alternative felt too heavy to carry.

I had been scammed.

And the worst part wasn't just the financial loss but the emotional cost. I had put my trust in a system that took advantage of my vulnerability. I had wanted so badly to believe that the long wait was over, that this was the beginning of something new.

Instead, it was a reminder of just how hard this season was turning out to be, and how important it would be to keep going anyway.

I had many painful experiences while trusting God for my ideal job, but this one, the scam, was perhaps the worst. I share it not to relive the pain, but to be transparent about how desperate I had become. I was discouraged. I was frustrated. And, honestly, I was mad at myself for being so trusting, and surprised that God, whom I knew could perform miracles in an instant, had allowed it to happen.

This is what we often don't talk about enough—what it feels like when you're doing your best to follow God and still hit a wall. When prayers go unanswered. When doors stay shut. When delay feels like denial.

In that season, I had one prayer:

"Lord, give me a job."

I said it in the morning.

I whispered it at night.

I cried it in the car, in church, while feeding my baby, while folding laundry.

It became the anthem of my life. It felt like the only thing I could possibly need.

Then one day, I felt God speak to my heart.

"You keep asking for this job like it's the only thing that matters. But to Me, your life is like a pie. The job is just one slice. I'm working on the other slices too. Pay attention to what else I'm doing."

That moment shifted everything.

I realized I had been so laser-focused on what I didn't have that I was missing what God was already doing. I was measuring His faithfulness by one prayer request. One job. One outcome. And I was forgetting that He saw the whole picture.

That moment taught me that sometimes, when God delays, it's not punishment, it's preparation.

He's not just answering your prayer.

He's shaping your life.

So, I began to pay attention.

And slowly, God started teaching me some lessons I hadn't asked for, but ones I desperately needed.

Your job is not your identity.

I didn't fully understand this until I no longer had a job. Up until then, my role as a software engineer at Altera had become more than a career. It had become how I saw myself. When we'd visit friends or attend events, I proudly introduced myself by my title. "Software engineer in the Bay Area" carried weight. My husband beamed every time he said, "My wife went to Cornell and works in San Jose." I wore that like a badge of honor.

Then we moved to Chicago.

Suddenly, I was nine weeks pregnant, unemployed, and navigating a new city while we planted a church. When people asked what I did, I didn't have the same answer or confidence. I was no longer "the woman in tech." I was just... a wife. A mom-to-be. And honestly, I wasn't one of those women who looked effortlessly radiant while pregnant. I was what you might call pregnant all over.

And while I knew that none of this should have affected my sense of worth, it did. The change shook something deep in me. I missed the subtle admiration in people's eyes when I mentioned my job. I missed how it made me feel about myself.

That's when I realized how tightly my identity had wrapped itself around a job title and a zip code. And God used that season to untangle it.

He reminded me that my identity isn't found in what I do or in what other people think of me. It's not rooted in LinkedIn bios, résumés, or casual introductions at dinner parties. My identity is in Him. In His approval. In His grace. Whether I had a job or not, whether anyone was impressed or not, I was still fully seen, fully loved, and completely accepted by God.

I had known that truth in theory for years. But in this season of waiting, it became real.

And it changed me. So that when the job eventually came, I was no longer looking for it to tell me who I was. I already knew.

Your job is not your source.

I always believed God was my provider. I said it. I taught it. I lived it. Until my paycheck started doing the talking for me.

After months of steady income at a great job in San Jose, I began to associate provision with stability, and stability with a job. There's nothing wrong with having a stable career. In fact, it's something we should all strive for. But at some point, my job stopped being what I did and became what I depended on. Without realizing it, I had started to see my job, not God, as my source.

And then, God stripped it away.

We were expecting our first child, and I had no idea how we were going to afford everything a baby required. The crib. The car seat. The endless list of things parents need. But then, almost quietly, provision started showing up. A gift here. An unexpected honorarium from one of my husband's ministry trips there, more than he had ever received at that point. We didn't live in excess, but we never went without. God covered every single need.

I also had to get creative. I remember standing in front of my closet, newly postpartum, staring at my Sunday clothes and thinking, *I have nothing to wear.* That became my weekly anthem. I didn't have the budget for new outfits, and that weighed on me more than I care to admit.

Then one day, I looked at the beautiful clothes I already owned, the ones I used to wear but couldn't fit into anymore, and something clicked. If I couldn't buy new clothes, maybe I could fit into the ones I already had. That became my motivation. I committed to losing the thirty-five pounds I had gained during pregnancy, not for vanity, but for practicality. And within weeks, I was back in my old outfits. That small win felt massive.

What I learned in that season was this: God doesn't just meet your needs through a paycheck. He uses people. He inspires generosity. He gives you creative solutions. And sometimes, He stretches you, not to punish you, but to remind you who the real source is.

Jobs are important. But they are not our source. God is. And He can be trusted, even when His timeline doesn't match ours.

Your blessing may look different from other people's.

During that season, I had to learn how to believe God for the basics—kitchen towels, bathroom curtains, even foot mats. It sounds simple, but when you're used to earning your own income, needing to pray for household essentials can feel deeply humbling.

There were times I'd visit someone's home and see the exact item I'd been praying for; maybe yellow kitchen towels I had imagined in my own kitchen, and there they were, freshly purchased in someone else's. I'd smile and say, "Lord, you delivered my towels to the wrong address."

This happened more than once. I'd see the bamboo foot mat I couldn't afford or the exact curtains I had clipped from a magazine, now hanging beautifully in someone else's bathroom. Every time, it stung. Not because I didn't want others to be blessed, but because it reminded me of what I didn't have.

God used those moments to work on my heart.

When someone else has what you've been praying for, it's easy to slip into comparison. It's easy to feel forgotten. But God was teaching me that covetousness, no matter how subtle, robs you of peace. It makes it hard to celebrate others. It creates distance where there could be connection. And worst of all, it blocks you from seeing the blessings that are showing up, even if they look different than you expected.

One of the most transformative lessons I learned at that time was learning to stop renting out mental real estate to other people's lives. What they had, what they wore, what they drove, and what they earned, were not mine to carry around on my mind. I had to make room in my mind and my heart for gratitude, not comparison.

And I needed that lesson more than I realized.

As our church began to grow, and we started pastoring people from all walks of life, including many with significant wealth and influence, I knew I couldn't lead well if I was secretly envying the people I was called to serve. True leadership starts with internal wholeness. You cannot pastor or lead with integrity if you're quietly resenting someone else's blessings.

Looking back, my early days in Chicago weren't what I had hoped for. I expected momentum, opportunity, progress. What I got instead were delays, detours, and long stretches of silence. But in those hidden places, I learned truths that have anchored me ever since.

God showed me that my identity isn't tied to a title. My provision doesn't come from a paycheck. And my blessing doesn't have to look like anyone else's.

These weren't just spiritual lessons, they were leadership lessons. They stripped away the things I thought made me valuable and replaced them with the things that *actually* do: character, trust, humility, and the courage to keep going when nothing is working the way you planned.

Eventually, the job came. But by then, I had already gained something far more important, a new foundation. A deeper sense of who I was. And the unshakable belief that no matter what season I find myself in, I am never forgotten, and I am never alone.

Five Lessons on Consecration from Chapter 5

1. **Who You Are Isn't What You Do**

    In Silicon Valley, I had a title that opened doors. "Software Engineer" wasn't just my job—it was part of my identity. When that title disappeared, so did the affirmation that came with it. I found myself in Chicago, pregnant and unemployed, unsure of how to introduce myself anymore.

That season taught me something I thought I already knew: identity isn't built on job titles or accolades. It's built on who you are when everything else is stripped away.

Consecration means letting go of the labels the world gives us and holding on to the truth that we are already valuable, already loved, without needing to earn it.

2. **Your Source Isn't a Paycheck**

   For months, I watched our savings shrink and my confidence with it. And then, when we had no backup plan, provision came, not from a job offer, but from unexpected gifts, timely honorariums, and resourcefulness that only God could have orchestrated.

   Consecration is learning to live like God actually is your source. Not your job. Not your degree. Not your network. It's scary. It's stretching. But it's also freeing. Because when the paycheck disappears, your Provider doesn't.

3. **Faith Is Also Found in the Waiting**

   I thought I would be unemployed for a few weeks, maybe a couple of months. It turned into a long, painful stretch of "no's" and "not yet's." And somewhere in that waiting room of life, I discovered something deeper than disappointment: trust.

   Trust that delay isn't denial. That closed doors can still lead you somewhere meaningful. That God doesn't just show up when things work out, He's shaping us *while* they don't.

   Consecration means staying faithful in the waiting, even when it feels like nothing is moving.

4. **Gratitude Doesn't Always Look Like Abundance**

   It's easy to say "thank you" when everything's going well. It's harder when you're believing God for kitchen towels while visiting friends who seem to have everything you're praying for.

   But in that space, between what I needed and what I had, God was working on my heart. He was teaching me to stop comparing and start seeing. Consecration is choosing contentment when you're tempted by comparison. It's celebrating others without resenting them. And it's trusting that your portion, even if small, is still sacred.

5. **There's Purpose Even in the Detour**

    The job didn't come when I wanted it to. But in the delay, something else was birthed; *my* first book, and later, a ministry to professionals. None of that was part of my plan. But it was clearly part of God's.

    Consecration is the courage to believe that where you are right now matters, even when it feels like a detour. Even when nothing looks like what you imagined. Because the place you didn't plan for might be the very ground where your purpose takes root.

6

Notable Miracles

My entire career has been shaped by moments I can only describe as miraculous. For a long time, I didn't even see them for what they were. I chalked it up to timing, luck, or persistence. But one day, my brother pointed it out to me that these moments, weren't typical. They weren't just chance. They were divine.

There was my admission to Cornell, which felt improbable at best. There was the unexpected $1,000 check from a stranger at a conference, an answer to a quiet prayer I hadn't dared to speak aloud. I've already shared some of those stories in this book. But in this chapter, I want to spotlight a few more of what you might call the quiet miracles, the ones that happened not just in mountaintop moments but in the valleys where faith is tested.

Because here's what I've learned: God cares deeply about our careers. He's not only present in the pews or the prayer closets, He shows up in boardrooms, interviews, and job applications, too. I've seen it firsthand.

Obeying God has never been my struggle. I can say yes. I can take the step. It's what happens after the obedience that often throws me off. It's the waiting. The discomfort. The gap between promise and fulfillment.

When we moved to Chicago, I was confident God would open the right door. I wasn't being called into full-time ministry like my husband. I believed I was still meant to work in the marketplace. And Jesus had made a promise in Mark 10—that anyone who left houses, family, or fields for the sake of the gospel would receive a hundredfold return.

I believed that promise. I had left a thriving tech job in California to help plant a church in a new city. I thought, *Surely the hundredfold is just around the corner.* But the job didn't come. Not right away. Not even close.

The real breakthrough came not long after I had our daughter. She was just two months old. I was in a familiar place again. A place of being qualified, jobless, and praying. I was doing everything I knew to do. Sending out resumes. Checking the few job boards that existed back then. Contacting recruiters. I had the right experience and the credentials to back it up. But nothing was working.

Then, during worship at a Sunday service, I heard God speak. Not audibly, but clearly. "Go back home, and I will show you how to write a resume."

At first, I brushed it off. That couldn't be God. It felt too…practical. Too ordinary. But two weeks later, the nudge came again, stronger this time. "When will you settle down and let Me show you how to write that resume?"

This time, I listened.

I went downstairs to the basement, sat at the computer, and opened a blank document. And then something happened. I didn't hear more words. I didn't see visions. But I had a mental image, clear and specific, of how the resume should look. Not just the format, but the flow. A structure that highlighted my skills right at the top. Bold headings. Categorized strengths. Rewritten experience descriptions tailored to each category.

No one was formatting resumes like that back then. Today, it's common. But at the time, it felt groundbreaking. I was seeing something ahead of its time, a divine download, as strange as that might sound. The resume wasn't exaggerated or embellished. It was simply laid out in a way that allowed my true value to shine through.

I sat there, amazed. Then I said, "Thank you." I saved the file, attached it to an email, and sent it to a recruiter.

And the miracle? It was already in motion.

About two weeks after I sent out my newly formatted resume, the phone rang.

It was a recruiter. "A company wants to interview you for a position," he said. "They have an opening for a Crystal Reports developer."

I paused. "Crystal Reports?" I'd never heard of it. I thanked him politely, hung up the phone, and panicked.

I didn't have Crystal Reports listed anywhere on my resume. Not even close. I had no idea what the job entailed. I opened my laptop, did a quick search, and found out it was a data reporting tool, something companies used to create business reports from databases. Think of it like Excel, but more dynamic and customizable. Okay. That gave me a starting point. Not enough to build a career on, but enough to Google.

I braced for the call from the hiring manager. I needed to prep fast.

But hours passed, and nothing happened.

After four long hours of overthinking, the recruiter finally called back. "They said they don't need to interview you," he said. "They want you to start on Monday."

Wait. What?

Who gets hired for a job they didn't apply for, in a skill they don't have, without an interview?

I was in the basement when I took the call. I raced upstairs and burst into the room where my husband was. "They just offered me a job," I said breathlessly. "They want me to start Monday. And I don't even know what the job is!"

We looked at each other in disbelief. After the Receiver Corporation scam, we weren't taking any chances. So we got in the car and drove to the company's listed address.

It was real.

Not only that—it was big. A well-established business with a proper building and actual signage. (Today, we would've just Googled it, but this was over sixteen years ago. No smartphones, no quick search.)

On the way home, reality sank in. "I don't know anything about Crystal Reports," I said. My husband, calm and steady, replied, "Then let's find a book."

We pulled into Barnes & Noble and picked up *Crystal Reports for Dummies*. That book became my lifeline.

The moment we got home, I dove in. I barely slept. I ran every example, clicked through every tutorial, and soaked in as much as I could. I had five days to learn an entirely new software tool—and zero margin for failure.

Then, on Thursday morning, the recruiter called again. "Change of plans.

They want you to start the following week. Your desk isn't ready yet."

Could I wait another week? Yes. Yes, I could.

The extra time felt like a gift from heaven. I used every minute to study, practice, and gain just enough confidence to fake it until I could back it up.

Then another call came the next Thursday. "Would you mind waiting one more week? Still no desk."

At this point, I didn't know what was going on with that desk, but I wasn't complaining. God had just bought me two full weeks of preparation time. When I finally walked into that company for my first day, I was nervous, yes, but I was also ready.

I walked in with my best work outfit on... and *Crystal Reports for Dummies* tucked discreetly into my bag.

The controller came down to meet me in the lobby. She shook my hand, smiled warmly, and said, "So, you're our new Crystal Reports expert."

I smiled right back. "Yes, ma'am."

And just like that, a miracle job I didn't apply for, in a skill I hadn't had three weeks earlier, became the next chapter in my career story.

My time at this company, a global leader in steel manufacturing, was nothing short of exciting. I had been home long enough and was eager to make the most of this opportunity. I came in as a temp-to-hire, and for me, it was the perfect chance to prove myself.

I threw myself into the role, and quickly, I was doing things with Crystal Reports that no one thought were possible. My first assignment was with the Accounting Department. The month-end reporting process was a mess; slow, repetitive, and redundant. I used my knowledge of both software development and Crystal Reports to develop templates that streamlined their processes. What used to take three weeks now took just three days. The accuracy of my reports was constantly validated, and the department was ecstatic.

Soon after, I was converted to a full-time employee. The pay was much higher, almost on par with my previous salary at Altera in California, minus the stock options. But it wasn't just the paycheck that made me feel validated. It was the recognition of how much I was contributing.

Then came a pivotal moment: The Head of IT from the headquarters in

Birmingham, Alabama, approached me with a game-changing offer. They wanted me to participate in a project implementing a business intelligence solution across twelve divisions of the company. I was one of only two people selected for the project. Shortly into it, the other person quit. But I didn't hesitate. I took on the challenge headfirst. I immersed myself in learning everything I could about the business intelligence solution, both front-end and back-end.

I also took on the task of educating people across the company about the value of business intelligence. I began to be referred to as the "business intelligence evangelist" at both my division and others.

Then, one day, out of the blue, my boss said, "Have you ever thought about starting your own company? If you start, we'll be your first client."

What?!! I was floored. You pray for miracles, but sometimes, they show up in ways you never expect. This was one of those moments that completely blindsided me. I had never imagined, planned, or even prayed for such an opportunity. It was more than I could ever ask for or think about.

But even though this new opportunity was incredible, I wasn't in a rush to leave my current role. I had grown close to my team, and I knew how valuable I was to them. After two years of driving fifty miles a day, after two back-to-back car accidents, I knew it was time for a change. My family and my ministry were becoming harder to balance with a long commute and a high-stress job.

I took a risk. I handed in my resignation letter. But it wasn't just a simple goodbye. I had written a letter that explained why I needed to leave, but also assured them I wasn't leaving them in the lurch. I hadn't secured another job yet, but I offered to stay on and help them find my replacement. I said I would train that person and only leave once they could confidently take over my role.

This was risky. I could've simply quit, and my boss could've said, "Okay, you're done." But I had faith. I knew I had built enough trust and had proven my value through the work I'd done that she wouldn't do that. We had a great working relationship, and I knew she would appreciate the care I took in handing over my responsibilities.

My boss was taken aback when she received the letter. "Let me think about it," she said. "I'll talk it over with Michelle." Michelle was the head of IT at the company's headquarters in Birmingham. My projects frequently involved collaboration with their central IT team, so this made sense.

What I didn't know at the time was how that conversation would change the trajectory of my career.

Three days later, my boss called me into her office. "We've thought about it," she said, "and we've decided we can't replace you. Have you ever thought of starting your own company?"

I couldn't believe it. She had just offered me a company! My initial reaction was a mix of thrill and disbelief. On the outside, I remained calm and composed. I knew my response could set the tone for any future negotiations. So, I told her I would think it over, left her office, and walked straight to my desk.

As soon as I sat down, I called my husband. "Babe, my boss just offered me a company!" I said, excitement spilling over. He was surprised but not entirely shocked. He had prophesied years before, while we were still in California, that I would one day own my own company. At the time, I hadn't seen how that could happen, so I had put the prophecy out of my mind. But now, it was all coming together.

We excitedly brainstormed about what we should name the company. And with that, the conversation ended with a single question: "What should we name it?"

After hanging up, I sat down with a pen and paper. I thought about the company and its origins. This was an opportunity that felt almost supernatural, an unexpected gift wrapped in business intelligence. I wanted the name to reflect a mix of the extraordinary and the practical.

I came up with "Divine Intelligence" to encapsulate both the divine nature of this opportunity and its focus on business intelligence. But I wanted to be subtle, so I shortened it to "Divintel." To make it even more unique, I swapped the first "i" with a "y," and just like that, Dyvintel was born.

The truth is, I never planned to start a company. Someone, or should I say a company, gave it to me. Most people spend years crafting a business plan, fine-tuning strategies, and laying the groundwork. But for me, this opportunity was unexpected, and as I reflected on it, I realized it was rooted in consecration.

Five years earlier, as I left my job in San Jose, I had clung to a scripture that anchored me during that season of transition. It was from Mark 10:29-30:

> *"So Jesus answered and said, 'Assuredly, I say to you, there is no one who has left house or brothers or sisters or father or mother or wife or children or lands, for My sake and the gospel's, who shall not receive a hundredfold now in this time—houses and brothers and sisters and mothers and children and lands, with persecutions—and in the age to come, eternal life.'" (NKJV)*

This promise of a hundredfold return was something I had held onto during the most challenging moments, and now, I saw it unfold in ways I hadn't imagined. It wasn't just the job or the salary—it was the opportunity to lead, to create, and to build something that aligned with my purpose.

Five Lessons on Consecration from Chapter 6

1. **Trusting Divine Guidance**

    Throughout my journey, the common thread has been my reliance on God's guidance, even when the path seemed unclear or daunting. From my miraculous admission to Cornell to the unexpected $1,000 check, there were moments that defied logic and explanation. These experiences remind me that true consecration involves trusting that God's plan for us is greater than anything we could imagine. It means believing that He will provide for us, even in the moments when things feel uncertain. Whether it's a career decision or a personal challenge, trusting in divine guidance requires a leap of faith, knowing that God's timing is always perfect, even when it doesn't align with our own.

2. **Obedience to God's Instructions**

    Sometimes, God's guidance doesn't make immediate sense—like when I felt nudged to rewrite my resume in a way no one had done before. It was a simple act of obedience, but it led to a job offer without an interview. This lesson has been central to my journey: consecration isn't just about following rules. It's about faithfully obeying God's instructions, even when they feel unconventional. It's about understanding that His wisdom surpasses ours, and trusting that the steps we take in obedience will lead to results beyond our understanding.

3. **Resilience in Adversity**
   There was no shortage of setbacks during my job search in Chicago. I waited months without a job, faced countless disappointments, and at times, felt deeply discouraged. But despite these challenges, I remained resolute in my faith. Consecration requires resilience; an unwavering commitment to continue pursuing God's purpose for us, even in the face of adversity. When things don't go according to plan, we have to remember that God is still at work, and the journey is just as important as the destination. The waiting isn't a sign of failure; it's a period of preparation and growth.

4. **God as the Source, Not the Job**
   In the midst of my career search, I had to reframe my understanding of provision. My job was not the source of my worth, nor was it the ultimate provider. God was. My experiences, whether they were the miraculous job offers or unexpected financial blessings, taught me that consecration involves recognizing that everything we need comes from God. It's not the job, the paycheck, or the position that defines us; it's our relationship with Him. Once I redefined my source, I was able to navigate career challenges with greater peace, knowing that God would provide in ways I couldn't predict or control.

5. **Living a Life of Integrity and Sacrifice**
   My decision to resign from a stable job in order to prioritize my family and support my husband in starting a church wasn't an easy one. But it was the right one. It taught me that true consecration is not just about career success or professional milestones, but about making choices that honor God and align with His will. Sometimes, the path to greater blessings requires personal sacrifice. When we prioritize our spiritual and familial commitments, we make room for God to bless us in ways we could never have planned. It's not just about what we gain, but also about living a life that reflects our values and serves others.

7

Mum at Work

Navigating motherhood and a career has been one of the most demanding experiences of my life, and yet, one of the most deeply transformative. I'm always grateful that I've had the opportunity to do both, though I often felt like I was constantly walking a tightrope. The arrival of my first child in March 2003, followed closely by my second in November 2004, marked a profound shift in my priorities. It reshaped my ambitions and completely remolded my daily routines.

My story differs slightly from that of many women who seek to combine motherhood with a challenging career. As someone who often sits in the front row of other people's lives, supporting, mentoring, and walking alongside them, I've seen firsthand the tension many women face trying to juggle it all. I deeply respect any woman who continues to put her best foot forward and shows up for herself and her family day after day. In my case, I wasn't working when I had both of my children, which made my journey unique in its way, and yet, it came with its complexities.

Reflecting on that time, I recognize that I had more flexibility than many mothers who must return to work shortly after childbirth. Some women return to work as early as two weeks postpartum simply because finances leave them no choice. We certainly felt the financial pinch during those seasons when I wasn't working, which was one reason I wanted to return to work as soon as possible. I did not enjoy working with such a tight budget. As my children grew, I wanted flexibility to cover the basics and provide more fully to enrich their lives, yes, but also to feel like I wasn't constantly scraping by.

In hindsight, not having a full-time job during the early years of my children's lives was a blessing in disguise, even if it didn't feel that way at the time. When we moved to Chicago, I was already pregnant with my son. I had hoped to land a job before his birth, but that didn't happen. Instead, I had the opportunity to spend several uninterrupted months with him before taking on a short-term contract. When that contract ended, I experienced another pause before getting a second one. During that time, I discovered I was expecting our daughter, and we also purchased our first home. The house was a considerable distance from the company where I was working. The long commute and modest pay made the job unsustainable, so I stepped away after some time.

What followed were months of restlessness. I wanted to work, contribute, and feel productive, but doors didn't open as quickly as I had hoped. That season was instrumental in confirming something I had long suspected: I was not called to be a stay-at-home mom. I didn't enjoy waking up with nowhere to go and no structured plan for the day. Perhaps it would have felt different if I had been working remotely, but I wasn't.

Looking back, I'm grateful for the time I spent with my children. But in that moment, I remember feeling so bored by repeating the same routine every day. I loved my children and genuinely enjoyed being with them, but I also longed for something more to keep my mind stimulated and my sense of purpose alive. I often wrestled with guilt for even having those thoughts. Shouldn't I have been content? But I wasn't, and I complained to my husband many more times than I should have.

Eventually, I got to spend four uninterrupted months with my daughter before, in what I can only describe as divine intervention, I secured my first full-time job in Chicago. It was nothing short of a miracle. As I've shared in an earlier chapter, I didn't interview for the job. I didn't even know the role beforehand. I was given two weeks to prepare and then stepped into a journey that would become pivotal for my career.

While I was grateful for the new job opportunity, the daily 50-mile commute each way, 100 miles round trip, quickly became a heavy burden. By 2007, I was stretched thin: commuting long hours, raising two young children, and supporting a growing church. The final straw came when I had two separate accidents, one year after the other, during snowstorms on my way home from work.

My route took me through remote farm roads where phone reception was often unreliable. One winter, I skidded off the road and into a ditch. Thankfully, someone was nearby and called a towing company to help pull me out. The following year, almost like déjà vu, it happened again. I managed to drive out of the ditch that time, but the experience shook me. I realized I didn't want to risk being stranded on those isolated back roads again, with no help in sight and no guarantee of safety.

Combined with the emotional and logistical weight I was already carrying, those incidents made it clear: something had to change. I was at a crossroads and had to make a pivotal decision. Eventually, I chose to resign from my job, a difficult but necessary step. I didn't realize then that this decision would open the door to something new. God's providence created space for an opportunity I hadn't even imagined: the chance to start my own company.

Quitting wasn't easy. I genuinely enjoyed the work and the people. But the stress had become unsustainable. I needed a path that offered flexibility without compromising purpose. And all that became possible through Dyvintel.

We started the company in the basement of our home. Soon after, we moved to a larger house where we finished the basement to serve as my office. The space was designed to accommodate my growing team of consultants, and I began training professionals in business intelligence and data analytics. Business grew steadily, and so did my confidence. But growth came with its tensions. I often questioned whether I was doing enough at home or doing too much at work. I wasn't just building a company; I was navigating the messiness of growth on every front.

During this time, we were also building a church. Though I wasn't on staff or formally employed by the ministry, the demands of that season were real and often invisible. There were counseling sessions that went long into the night, impromptu meetings that pulled my husband away at crucial moments, and his travel schedules that left me managing things solo more often than I liked. Having a consecrated heart helped me in these times. It helped me to focus on the fact that God had a plan and a calling on our lives that we were both honoring in our unique ways. Sometimes I felt alone, stretched thin, not just by parenting and work but also by the hidden load of ministry.

But the truth is that I wasn't alone. My husband helped run Dyvintel. He was involved in the decisions on who to hire next, and even though we weren't big enough to have a human resources department, he was in charge of employee morale and payroll. It also meant much to me when he stepped in and took over at home when I had to travel. Those gestures made space for me to grow, too.

Working from home brought a new rhythm to my life. I was present when my children came home from school, able to help with homework, share meals, and return to work as needed. Yet, maintaining boundaries was a constant challenge. Teaching my children to respect my work hours required patience and persistence. Some days they got it, and some days, they didn't. And honestly, some days, I didn't either.

Summer became a sacred time, but even then, I often struggled to fully disconnect from work. I prayed for lighter client loads and enrolled my kids in programs that nurtured their minds, bodies, and spirits. When they were home, I gave them "mommy work" to keep them engaged while I tackled deadlines. It was beautiful and exhausting. And some days, I was more present than others.

Running a consulting business also came with frequent travel, which required meticulous planning and, honestly, a lot of emotional energy. My husband stepped in when I was away, doing things in his own unique way. Letting go of control was hard. I had to learn to accept help, even when it didn't come in the exact form I would have preferred. That lesson was humbling, but invaluable.

My mother was an incredible blessing during those years. Her steady presence, especially after my father passed, made it easier for me to focus on my business without constantly worrying about my children. Church members, particularly the young ladies I mentored, also played a significant role. We created a system where I supported them through mentorship, and they supported me with childcare. It wasn't perfect, but it allowed us all to grow together.

As my children grew older, I became more intentional about surrounding them with trusted adults who could mentor and guide them in ways I couldn't always do on my own. This is a subject I hope to explore more deeply in a future book on parenting.

Even with a growing business, I made it a priority to stay engaged in my children's lives. Of course, I missed things—events, school activities, little moments that made me wish I could clone myself. But I made it to many of them. I focused especially on their emotional wellness. While I couldn't control their experiences or how they felt about them, I worked hard to ensure they knew I was there for them and that they could talk to me. It wasn't always balanced, but it was always honest. I did my best.

Despite the hurdles, I learned to navigate the delicate tension between motherhood and leadership. It wasn't perfect; there were missed milestones, last-minute cancellations, and moments of guilt that lingered longer than I would've liked. But I kept moving forward, fueled by the belief that both motherhood and entrepreneurship were part of my divine assignment.

Balancing work, family, and other responsibilities will require intentionality. It's not an easy feat, but it is possible. Here are five key strategies to help you stay grounded and navigate the complex demands of work and motherhood:

1. **Prioritizing and Planning:** Careful planning is essential to managing competing responsibilities without burning out. Break larger goals into smaller, actionable tasks, and set clear boundaries to help you stay focused. If you don't always stick to them perfectly, remember to give yourself grace. Progress matters far more than perfection.

2. **Seeking and Accepting Support:** You don't have to do it all alone. Embrace help from your spouse, extended family, friends, or church community. Let go of the pride that tells you asking for help is a sign of weakness. It's not. It's wisdom, and it's what will sustain you long term.

3. **Embracing Flexibility:** Things won't always go as planned, and that's okay. Flexibility is your greatest ally. Whether that means working at unconventional hours or rearranging your schedule last-minute, allow yourself the room to adjust. This flexibility is what will make space for you to be fully present when it matters most.

4. **Fostering Focus and Discipline at Home:** Teach your children

responsibility early on. Establish simple routines, encourage creative projects, and make space for shared quiet work time. It won't always be perfect, but it will help you and your family grow together and keep things running smoothly at home.

5. **Prioritizing Self-Care:** This is likely the hardest of all. But you must make time for yourself. Rest, nourish your spirit, and allow for moments of stillness and mental clarity. These are not luxuries. They're survival tools. When you're well-rested and recharged, everything else flows more smoothly.

By embracing these strategies, you'll be able to lead with balance, grace, and purpose, thriving in both your professional and personal life.

Your road won't always be smooth. There will be tears, doubt, and days when you feel like walking away from it all. But every challenge will shape you. Each setback will refine your purpose. And every small win, whether it's closing a deal, showing up for a school event, or simply getting through a tough day, will remind you that you are doing meaningful, purposeful work.

You don't need to get it all right. You just have to keep going. One faithful step at a time.

The road hasn't always been smooth for me. There were tears, second-guessing, and days when I wanted to give up. But every setback shaped me, and each challenge refined my purpose. Every small win, whether in my work or with my kids, reminded me that this path, however winding, was mine.

Now that my children are grown and both in college, I look back with a mix of gratitude and reflection. There are certainly things I wish I had done differently, but the truth is, I'm just glad I kept showing up. I'm proud of the adults they are becoming, and I'm deeply grateful for who they are. I'm also glad they saw me striving for more, not perfection, but purpose. I believe it's inspired them in their own journeys.

Life rarely unfolds in predictable patterns. These days, I focus on rhythm; an ebb and flow that allows me to be fully present where I'm most needed. Sometimes that means leaning into work, other times it's about ministry, family, my husband, or simply taking time for myself.

I don't have it all figured out. I still wrestle with questions. I still feel the pull of competing priorities. But I've learned to anchor myself in grace for the days I show up strong, and grace for the days I just show up.

To every woman balancing motherhood and ambition, know this: you are not alone. You are not behind. Your efforts matter, even when they feel unseen. Your story is sacred. Your sacrifices are seeds for a desirable future. And though the road may be uneven, it is deeply meaningful. Keep showing up. One faithful step at a time.

8

The Only (Black) Woman in the Room

When I entered the Electrical and Electronics Department at Obafemi Awolowo University, Ile-Ife, in 1992, I was one of only three women in a cohort of around one hundred students. The other two and I quickly bonded, finding camaraderie in each other's company. We were a small group of friends amidst what seemed like a sea of young men who did not look like us or handle the stress of academic rigor like us. It felt isolating many times, but our bond helped me to navigate what would have otherwise been a much more stressful situation. It wasn't that the men mistreated us. They were sometimes too loud, sometimes too energetic, but they were always decent to us.

Recently, during a television interview, I was asked why women in male-dominated fields like engineering or physics sometimes struggle or ultimately leave, despite having equal opportunities. My interviewer shared an example from his own university days, recalling two women who had eventually dropped out of his physics program without any clear external pressures. He wondered why equal access didn't guarantee their success. I explained to him that while equality, like gaining admission, is a critical first step, equity is the essential second step. Equity recognizes the hidden, deeper challenges that arise from being "one of the few," and it provides the resources and support to address them.

Admission to Obafemi Awolowo University(OAU) as one of the few women in Electrical and Electronics gave me an equal standing to succeed as the men. However, beyond equality lies equity, which delves deeper into other issues, often hidden beneath the surface, that affect people's ability to reach their full potential. Although I thrived in my department at OAU, it was in the face of the challenges that came with being a minority in a male-dominated class.

Here is a practical way that emotions of loneliness can affect a person's ability to succeed. Let us go back to the example presented by my TV interviewer. A course like physics is very challenging (in fact, there is no college-level course that is not challenging). Imagine it's late at night, and one of those ladies has difficulty completing an assignment due the next day. It is too late to leave her dorms for safety considerations or some other reason. She has only one other person who could help her out, who would be the second girl in her class. Let's go to the men's dorm and imagine that scenario. A male counterpart in that class has many more options than his female classmate. That is just one example of how loneliness can have far-reaching consequences, even though it sounds like an emotion. Courses are conquered one difficult assignment at a time. Equality put those two ladies in the same class as the men. However, equity would consider other inhibiting factors and help them overcome those so they could truly have the same chances at success.

My time at Obafemi Awolowo University lasted until 1995, when I transferred to the Electrical Engineering program at the University of Oklahoma, Norman. I wasn't prepared to be one of the few women, and the only Black woman, in my department. I wasn't prepared for being black in America. I had never been so conscious of the color of my skin in my entire life. I was self-conscious of being different.

That kind of self-consciousness is something I work very hard against now, in my adult years. It has a crippling effect on your creative expression, your spontaneity, and it erodes your confidence. Many things can create this self-consciousness, even when it is not provoked in us by others. The bottom line is, in 1995, I suddenly became more self-conscious than ever.

Realizing how easily self-consciousness could undermine me, I knew I needed a clear, powerful motivation to anchor my efforts. I decided to focus on making my parents proud—they were thousands of miles away in Nigeria, rooting for my success. Their hopes became my North Star, pushing me to give my absolute best in every class.

My years at Obafemi Awolowo University instilled in me a discipline that became foundational. The demanding coursework quickly taught my friends and me to focus less on how we differed from our peers and more on how we could excel. We didn't dwell on feeling outnumbered; instead, we made academic excellence our shared culture. When I transferred to the University of Oklahoma, I carried this mindset with me.

I put my head down, poured myself into my studies, and soon my effort spoke louder than any biases my professors might have had about my gender or skin color. It became clear to everyone, including myself, that exceptional performance was the strongest equalizer. My grades left no room for doubt: I belonged, and I was more than capable of holding my own.

As an international student, my accent quickly became another reason to feel self-conscious. Being naturally introverted made social interactions challenging enough, and having to repeat myself constantly only added to my discomfort. Often, I chose silence over the embarrassment of being misunderstood.

To overcome this, I actively sought communities where I felt less pressure—places where my differences were shared experiences, not isolating ones. Joining groups like the African Students Association, the African Christian Fellowship, and the International Students Association gave me a much-needed sense of belonging. In these spaces, I found peers navigating similar journeys, and suddenly, being different didn't mean feeling alone.

If I could have squeezed more time in my day, I would have joined two other organizations at the University of Oklahoma. The first was the National Society of Black Engineers. They are a national organization that creates opportunities for Black engineers. They help them overcome systems of bias that would have prevented these engineers from staying in their programs or getting access to so many opportunities. The second was the Society of Women Engineers, which does something similar for women in engineering. There is still a lot of work to be done, but these organizations have done a great job of providing a community for minorities in the Engineering field. They help keep people who feel "different" due to their skin color in fields that they may otherwise leave due to a lack of encouragement or adequate representation.

I still check in on what's going on at the University of Oklahoma from time to time. I have seen the African population on campus increase over time. I have had the opportunity to form friendships with other black people who graduated years after I did. I imagine they had unique experiences, but the feeling of isolation may not have been as severe for them. I am delighted by that progress and the opportunity that diversity affords people, especially those leaving their home countries, to study far away from home.

My program at Cornell University was fast-paced, and I had little time for social activities outside of my schoolwork. However, I had four other African-American women in my engineering program. They had all come from the same company and already had a relationship, but they were kind enough to let me into their circle. It was a professional master's program, and I would have benefited from a more practical background with more professional experience, which I did not have. I sometimes struggled with the expectations of having more hands-on experience. My strong theoretical foundation from Nigeria made me better suited to courses focused on theory. I often wished there had been more people like me—people I could turn to for help. My four new friends felt the same way. Engineering is hard, and group work is critical. So, it is always beneficial to have more people wanting you to be in their groups or wanting to pair up with you. And when you struggle with a concept, it doesn't help to see in the other person's eyes that they weren't expecting you to know it anyway. I was always happy to prove people wrong and earn their respect at the University of Oklahoma. But at Cornell, I struggled a little bit more with that. The material was more challenging, and I did not have many people to turn to for help who I felt would not bruise my ego.

My first job out of graduate school felt like the moment I was most acutely aware of my difference. I longed for deep connections and friendships where I could share experiences, but I often felt like the only one of my kind in many corporate settings. I didn't have the kind of casual conversations others did. Many times, I found myself eating lunch alone. I focused on doing my job to the best of my ability, but it was a lonely experience. My coworkers didn't intend to make me feel isolated. They probably didn't know how much I struggled with wanting to belong, wishing more people would go out of their way to form deeper connections with me. I was much younger then and didn't have the skills to initiate friendships. I just sat alone and wished things were different.

To anyone in a position to help others feel included: show that you are genuinely interested in them. Don't ask awkward questions they probably get from everyone else, like, "Where is your accent from? I like it." That phrase is overused. Try to avoid it. A person with an accent already knows they sound different from others. Pointing it out makes them feel more self-conscious. Acknowledge something about them that you genuinely admire, try to make them feel included, and don't just highlight what makes them stand out.

Having a unique name has undoubtedly created its fair share of awkward moments throughout my life, both in school and in my professional career. My full name is Olumayowa, which means "God has brought us joy," and the short form is Mayowa, meaning "to bring joy." I've always preferred going by my first name because it feels integral to who I am. Though I have an English middle name, Abigail, I've always felt that Mayowa is the name that truly represents me.

Introducing myself became an exercise in humor. I would explain, "It's M in front of Iowa—M-IOWA." Sharing this insight would usually lighten the mood, allowing people to relax, laugh, and feel more comfortable pronouncing my name correctly. In many ways, I learned to use the uniqueness of my name to create a connection. It became a conversation starter, an icebreaker.

Handling the feeling of being different came down to what I focused on. I decided early on that my work would be my equalizer. I didn't want to be judged based on my name, gender, or race—so I let the quality of my work speak for itself. At the same time, I leaned on principles I sincerely believed in, particularly scriptures like I Corinthians 13:4-8, which have always guided me in life and in relating with people.

> *Love endures long and is patient and kind; love never is envious nor boils over with jealousy, is not boastful or vainglorious, does not display itself haughtily. It is not conceited (arrogant and inflated with pride); it is not rude (unmannerly) and does not act unbecomingly. Love (God's love in us) does not insist on its own rights or its own way, for it is not self-seeking; it is*

> *not touchy or fretful or resentful; it takes no account of the evil done to it [it pays no attention to a suffered wrong]. It does not rejoice at injustice and unrighteousness, but rejoices when right and truth prevail. Love bears up under anything and everything that comes, is ever ready to believe the best of every person, its hopes are fadeless under all circumstances, and it endures everything [without weakening]. Love never fails [never fades out or becomes obsolete or comes to an end]. (AMPC)*

I paid attention to walking in my identity in Christ Jesus, especially during those times when feelings of being different would almost overwhelm me and make me shrink back in cowardice. I would remind myself that I am the righteousness of God in Christ. To me, being righteous means that if I can stand before God, the creator of all men and all races, without a sense of inferiority, then I can stand in front of anyone and do work or business with them regardless of my gender or skin color. I would often practice saying this to myself repeatedly, maybe in the restroom, before a business meeting or a particularly challenging project.

There is significant injustice in the world, particularly affecting people of color. We must continue to address these issues and the systems that perpetuate or protect inequality. The journey has been long, and much remains to be accomplished. I have always been aware of this. Simultaneously, I recognized that as we advocated for broader change, I needed to accept the truth of my identity as defined in Scripture. I discovered numerous biblical examples of individuals who overcame adversity and succeeded, even gaining recognition in foreign territories.

An example is Joseph. Joseph was an enslaved person who was probably naked when he was sold in the slave market to Potiphar. Despite his unfortunate circumstances, he did exceptional work in Potiphar's house. God was with him and caused everything he did to prosper. Within a short time, Potiphar promoted him to the head of his house. He was like the executive director. Potiphar's wife set him up. She wanted him to sleep with her. When he refused, she lied and said he had tried to take advantage of her. Potiphar was so mad that he imprisoned Joseph without access to a fair trial.

Potiphar intended to have him rot there. However, even in prison, Joseph excelled. He stood out, and the prison manager recognized him. Joseph made some crucial connections in prison. One in particular, the King's butler, was responsible for the recommendation that led to him becoming prime minister. You don't need everyone on your side; you just need the right people. You don't need everyone to like you. You just need the right people to like you. I have always encouraged myself with the story of Joseph whenever I felt different, especially when I felt my difference would be a disadvantage. I have often told myself that I am made the way I am for God's purpose, and the world systems must recognize that.

Another story I usually encourage myself with is the story of Daniel. Daniel had been captured and taken to Babylon along with multitudes of other Israelites when King Nebuchadnezzar besieged Jerusalem. He was in a strange land, not even a citizen. He did not belong. But God was faithful to Daniel. Daniel found favor in the eyes of his immediate supervisor and even the overall boss, the King. He was chosen to be a part of an accelerator program because of the aptitude he already possessed. That is why it's essential to develop competence, even when it doesn't seem like you need it. Daniel was chosen to participate in this program with three other friends and many other young Hebrew boys. Even in captivity, Daniel remained faithful to his covenant with God.

All the people in Daniel's cohort were supposed to engage in specific practices as part of the program, contrary to his conviction and covenant with God. Daniel politely requested to be exempted from these practices. He could have been kicked out of the program for this, but his confidence in God was not misplaced. God delivered on that confidence. Daniel and his friends did very well at the exit interview at the end of the program and were highly placed in the King's realm. Daniel continued to prosper throughout his career, and he ended up working under four different kings. I have encouraged myself throughout my career with this story and other accounts of Daniel's life and the many supernatural things that happened while he served his bosses faithfully but with deep conviction based on his covenant with God. It didn't matter that Daniel was different. It didn't matter that people did not even like him. Even when he was conspired against, God gave him the upper hand. In his case, he was a Jewish man in Babylon, the most powerful nation at that time. His people were despised in Babylon, but God had something to prove through Daniel's life, and He did.

God has something to prove through your life. We are His workmanship created in Christ Jesus unto good works which He planned before for us to walk in. That is one of the things that excites me the most about Christians engaging with the marketplace. It allows God to defy all odds throughout our lives. Racism or sexism may be what you are dealing with. Yes, these issues should be dealt with at the systemic level, but in the meantime, you can create an exemption for yourself by developing your confidence in what God can do, even when men don't want it for you. Reading and meditating on stories like Daniel's can help you develop that confidence.

I want to take a moment to address the "different" Black person phenomenon, particularly for women of color. When you stand out because you've done the hard work through discipline, faith, and purpose, people may begin to see you as "different." This phenomenon happens when, despite the stereotypes and biases, your competency breaks through the barriers people have erected. For example, when someone thinks, "I've always thought Black people were incompetent, but I see she is competent, even though she is Black," you might hear, "She's a different Black person." The reality is that just because we succeed individually, it doesn't automatically dismantle the biases others have. We must work actively to change that narrative for others.

To truly move the needle for those who come after us—so they don't have to fight the same battles—we need to give back. We can do this by fighting oppression and bias or, more personally, empowering others to break free from prejudice and limiting beliefs. I have chosen to empower others.

Over the years, I have organized many empowerment programs for women of color to help us think better about ourselves. I have done so under the umbrella of women's conferences, where we have explored themes like:

- **Digging for Virtue:** We talked about not just waiting for people to discover your worth but doing the hard work of digging deep enough (deeper than your gender or skin color) to find treasures stored up in you so you can bring them out for others to see.

- **Options:** We talked about the fact that you have options. If one door closes, you don't have to despair. Examine the other options you have. Never give up. Keep moving forward.
- **Exposure:** You need to see beyond what is in your current horizon. Your exposure will either give you wings or ground you. We examined how women can gain the exposure they need to move forward and achieve more.

I have hosted these conferences and mentored many individuals, helping them understand how to lead consecrated and successful careers. When I ran my company, Dyvintel, I made it a point to empower immigrants with technical backgrounds just starting their careers. I provided training in business intelligence, helping many discover their potential in a field they had not considered before.

Helping others shift their perspective can be one of the most powerful tools we have to confront inequality. When we empower people to see themselves differently—to recognize their own strength and potential—we not only lift them up, but we also weaken the hold of bias and discrimination. Real progress happens when we enable others to reframe their limitations into possibilities, creating a cycle of empowerment that benefits everyone.

From the beginning of my college education at the Obafemi Awolowo University, Ile-Ife, through my time in Silicon Valley to my time in full-time ministry and back to my involvement in the marketplace, I have realized that success that is focused on just breaking barriers for myself is limiting. Those who are truly successful and fulfilled are committed to breaking barriers for themselves and investing in others' successes. I have received so much help in my journey, especially through those times when I have felt lonely as the only woman, the only black person, or the only black woman in the room. Through my two friends in my electrical engineering program, the organizations where I found companionship on campus, and the encouragement I drew from the stories of biblical heroes like Daniel and Joseph, my journey has been shaped beautifully over the years. And now, through mentorship and dedication to creating spaces for growth, I have worked to pay it forward for community progress and success. I desire that my life is never truly just about me, but that every difficult thing I push myself to overcome will show others what is possible and create teaching opportunities to show others what can be done.

Five Lessons on Consecration from Chapter 8

1. **Embrace Your Identity in Christ**

    My identity in Christ helps me navigate my challenges with being different or the isolation those challenges may cause. When I felt "different," I tried not to meditate on that but to let my mind get overwhelmed by the fact that I am the righteousness of God in Christ Jesus. Consecration is about making your identity in Christ core to your sense of self-worth or belonging. You belong in Christ. Nothing beats that.

2. **Perseverance in the Face of Adversity**

    My journey has been full of moments where I was the only woman or person of color in a room, but I learned that perseverance is key. Like Joseph, who prospered despite being wrongfully imprisoned, I focused on my work and let excellence be my equalizer. Consecration means not allowing circumstances to dictate your progress. Even when faced with adversity, trust that God will honor your diligence and open doors for you, no matter how challenging the environment. Success results from continuing to press forward, even when the path is unclear.

3. **Commitment to Excellence**

    Throughout my education and career, I used my performance to defy stereotypes and prove my value. Excellence isn't just about your work—it's about using your talents to testify to God's work in you. Consecration means dedicating every effort to God, letting Him guide and empower you to achieve greatness. Striving for excellence is a form of worship, demonstrating that God is working through you to fulfill His purpose.

4. **The Power of Focus and Discipline**

    There were many moments in my life when I felt out of place, whether due to my accent, gender, or background. But during those moments, I learned the importance of focus and discipline. I had to focus on the bigger picture—my goals, faith, and calling—and trust that my commitment would carry me through. Like Daniel, who maintained his faith in a foreign land despite immense pressure, I stayed disciplined in my pursuit of excellence. Consecration means staying focused on your mission, no matter the distractions around you, and remaining disciplined to honor God through your work.

5. **Empowering Others through Mentorship**
Through mentorship, I have been able to help people like me overcome limiting beliefs, show them how to navigate biases, and how to find their voice. Consecration involves dedicating yourself to God and empowering others along the way. Your success is a tool for creating opportunities for those who come after you. Investing in others helps build a cycle of growth and empowerment that transforms entire communities.

9

Sacrificing Isaac: Leaving for Full-Time Ministry

In September 2017, I received a calling that would shift the course of my life. God told me it was time to move into full-time ministry. As with many of the pivotal moments in my journey, this direction came when I least expected it. It didn't happen in a formal setting; it wasn't during a church service or prayer meeting. I've come to realize that God can speak to us at any time, in any place. We just have to be open to listening. He is a Father who desires to connect with His children wherever they are. We often try to box God in, but He is limitless in how He can speak to us.

It was during a casual conversation at a friend's house, celebrating the birth of their baby, when I heard God speak. This was a business discussion, something we had often shared as we exchanged ideas about growth and profitability in our businesses. But in the middle of our conversation, I heard God's voice clearly: "You've been asking the wrong question. What if I told you that it's time? It's time; I need you in ministry full-time."

I didn't fully understand what He meant by "the wrong question." I had often wondered, "When is the right time to transition into full-time ministry?" But this moment was unmistakable: God had given me clear direction; it was time to shift. This wasn't just a career change; it had profound implications. I would be closing my business, joining my husband in our work at The Apostolic Place, and contributing to the global ministry we had been building together.

At that time, I had already moved my business out of my basement and into a commercial office building in Northbrook, Illinois. Telling my landlord that

I would be closing my office was a moment of clarity. He was supportive and not at all surprised. He said something that stuck with me: "You're finally going after your greatest passion; serving God full-time." It was humbling to hear this, and it dawned on me just how evident my passion for ministry had been, even in the midst of running a business.

I closed the office at the end of December 2017, donated my office furniture and computers to the church, and prepared for the next chapter with God. The logistical part of closing down my business was relatively straightforward, but the emotional transition was much more complex. Shifting my focus and identity from the corporate world to full-time ministry was a deeper, more difficult change. Even though I had taken the steps to obey, I still longed for the marketplace for at least two years. I found myself browsing LinkedIn to see what was happening in the business world, staying up-to-date with emerging technologies, and wondering about potential job opportunities.

What I didn't realize at the time was that I was keeping a safety net, an escape route back to my old life in case ministry didn't work out. I was unwilling to let go completely, even though I had made the external changes. It wasn't until two years later, when I truly surrendered my heart, that I fully aligned myself with what God had called me to do. It was like the story of Lot's wife who moved physically but kept looking back, stuck in the past. I had to stop looking back to fully embrace the future God had in store for me.

When I finally let go of the corporate world mentally, emotionally, and spiritually, I began to experience the blessings and growth that came with fully stepping into the calling God had for me.

As I transitioned into full-time ministry, I began to view my work as an opportunity for career growth in a completely new dimension. While my previous roles had been deeply rooted in technology, software engineering, business intelligence, and data analytics, my primary identity had been as a technical person. My focus had been on developing complex systems, analyzing data, and optimizing processes. But ministry opened up a whole new world for me, one that required a different set of skills, centered around organizational leadership and people management.

The fellowship my husband, Kayode, started at Obafemi Awolowo University in Ile-Ife had grown into a global ministry with churches across Africa, Europe, and North America. Our church in Chicago served as the headquarters, and I stepped into the role of Executive Vice President of Strategy and resident pastor. This was a shift from the technical work I had done in the past. It required strategic thinking, the ability to lead with empathy, and a deep understanding of spiritual leadership. It was no longer just about systems or data; it was about people—helping them grow, providing them with support, and inspiring them to align with a higher purpose.

In 2018, I completed my Executive Scholar Certificate in Nonprofit Management. This program equipped me with essential skills in areas like fundraising, financial management, and organizational development tailored to the unique needs of nonprofit and faith-based organizations. I learned how to develop sustainable programs, manage diverse teams, and create strategies that generated impact. These lessons were invaluable as I navigated the complexities of leading a growing ministry and managing global initiatives. The ability to apply these strategies helped us expand our outreach, increase community engagement, and ensure our operations ran smoothly.

The most fulfilling aspect of my role became working with people. I realized that every interaction was an opportunity to unlock someone's potential and make a real difference in their lives. Leading a diverse congregation and a team of volunteers required patience, empathy, and the ability to listen actively. I focused on creating a supportive environment where individuals felt seen and empowered to use their unique gifts. This included holding one-on-one meetings and leading group training sessions. By investing in their growth, I saw how it benefited not only the individuals involved but also the ministry as a whole.

People development became the cornerstone of my leadership approach. I firmly believed that everyone has unique strengths that, when nurtured, could help them thrive. Identifying these strengths and creating opportunities for growth became a key priority. We established mentorship programs, leadership training, and continuous education initiatives that empowered individuals to build confidence and expand their skill sets. Seeing volunteers and team members transform as they discovered their potential and embraced greater responsibilities was one of the most fulfilling aspects of my role.

Leadership development was not just about cultivating individuals but ensuring the sustainability of our ministry. We needed strong leaders who could carry the vision forward. I worked closely with emerging leaders, offering coaching, feedback, and hands-on opportunities to take charge of projects and initiatives. This blend of practical experience and formal leadership training helped these leaders develop the skills and self-assurance needed to lead effectively. We fostered a culture of servant leadership, where leaders prioritized the needs of others, led by example, and worked to uplift those around them.

Volunteer management was another critical area that demanded strategic thinking. Volunteers were the backbone of our ministry, and their commitment was essential to our success. I made it a priority to ensure that volunteers felt engaged, valued, and aligned with our mission. This was achieved through consistent communication, recognition, appreciation events, and a structured feedback system. By cultivating a positive volunteer experience, we ensured high levels of satisfaction and retention, which ultimately strengthened our ministry's impact.

Nurturing people's potential was an ongoing process. It required creating an environment where individuals felt safe to explore new opportunities, take on challenges, and learn from their mistakes. We encouraged a growth mindset where setbacks were viewed as learning experiences, not failures. By providing training, resources, and a supportive community, we allowed people to flourish. The results were evident in the personal growth of individuals and the collective progress of our ministry.

At the heart of everything we did was a commitment to caring for people. We sought to build a community where every individual felt seen, heard, and valued. Pastoral care programs, support groups, and counseling services were integral to addressing the diverse needs of our congregation. We focused on fostering strong relationships, creating a sense of belonging, and offering support through every challenge. Whether offering a listening ear, providing practical help, or delivering a word of encouragement, we worked to reflect Christ's love in all our interactions. This holistic approach to ministry didn't just support individual growth, it strengthened the fabric of our church and helped it flourish as a unified community.

Two and a half years after leaving the marketplace, God introduced me to a new ministry, *Dear Pastor's Wife*, which became another layer of responsibility, passion, and purpose on top of my ongoing commitments.

The journey began with the book *Dear Pastor's Wife*, which I wrote during the 2020 pandemic. The process of writing the book felt like divine timing, as I was led to find a writing coach who was not only a seasoned professional but also a pastor's wife herself. She understood my mission and vision for the book in a way that made the process feel natural and aligned with God's plan for me. That coach was Laju Iren, whose guidance was instrumental in shaping *Dear Pastor's Wife* into what it is today.

The book resonated deeply with women who were married to pastors, ministers, or men with a strong sense of calling. The response was so overwhelming that I felt a deep responsibility to steward what God had entrusted to me. This led me to launch initiatives under the *Dear Pastor's Wife* banner, including events designed to celebrate pastors' wives during Pastors' Wives Appreciation Month, tea parties in cities across the country, educational webinars, a leadership conference, and a benefit gala aimed at raising awareness of the importance of supporting pastors' wives.

Running *Dear Pastor's Wife* has been one of the most demanding, impactful, and rewarding undertakings of my life. It has stretched me in new ways and deepened my commitment to empowering women in ministry. I was not just serving in a pastoral role; I was actively building a platform to uplift and support women in unique and challenging positions—those who often give so much but receive so little recognition.

When I stepped into full-time ministry, I never imagined that God would eventually call me back to the marketplace. I thought that chapter had closed for good. But as with many of God's plans, I learned that His timing and direction are not always what we expect. What began as a season of dedication to ministry turned into a pivotal moment in which I found myself being led back to the marketplace. A space I had once left behind. The call back to the marketplace is one that is shaping my journey in ways I couldn't have foreseen.

Five Lessons on Consecration from Chapter 9

1. **Obedience to Divine Timing**
Transitioning into full-time ministry in 2017 was a life-changing moment that underscored the importance of responding to God's timing. Sometimes, we may feel like we're on the right track, but divine timing often calls us to step out of our comfort zones at unexpected moments. Consecration requires us to listen for God's voice and trust that His timing, even when it disrupts our own plans, leads to something greater than we can foresee. Obedience in this context was more than a career shift—it was a step toward fulfilling God's ultimate purpose for my life.

2. **Letting Go and Fully Committing**
Consecration calls for a full surrender of our old ways, identities, and attachments. It was one thing to close my business physically, but the true work came when I released my emotional and mental attachment to the corporate world. For two years, I struggled with letting go, keeping an escape route in mind in case ministry didn't work out. But when I fully committed and stopped looking back, that's when I began to experience the growth and fulfillment I had longed for. Full surrender is often a slow, internal process, but it's the gateway to seeing God's will unfold in unexpected, beautiful ways.

3. **Embracing New Roles and Responsibilities**
The shift from technical roles in the corporate world to leadership in ministry was a profound leap, and it required not only new skills but a new mindset. Consecration means embracing the unknown and trusting that God equips us for every new responsibility, even when it stretches us beyond what we thought we were capable of. Whether it's leading with empathy, making strategic decisions, or guiding others spiritually, this shift was a testament to the fact that God can use us in unexpected roles if we stay open to His calling..

4. **Investing in People Development**
As I transitioned into ministry, I learned that true leadership is rooted in empowering others. Mentorship, leadership training, and creating

opportunities for personal and professional growth became central to my role. Consecration isn't just about our personal growth but about fostering the growth of those around us. It's about creating spaces where others can flourish, just as I was given the space to grow. This is what ministry and leadership truly look like: investing in people so that they can carry the vision forward.

5. **Caring for the Community**

    Ministry, at its core, is about people; caring for them, serving them, and walking with them through life's challenges. The initiatives I launched through *Dear Pastor's Wife* were a direct expression of consecration, as I sought to meet the unique needs of pastors' wives who often serve in silence. It's about seeing the individual in the crowd, meeting them where they are, and offering care, healing, and community. Consecration is about building relationships, fostering connection, and making sure that everyone feels seen, heard, and valued.

10

Getting Isaac Back

I thought I was done with my "career." But in God's plan, "career" was far from finished with me. I never expected that my time in full-time ministry was preparing me for what would come next—a return to the marketplace, but this time, in a larger capacity and with greater authority. The story of how this unfolded is still in progress, but here's how it began.

It started with a chance encounter at a birthday party. I met a former colleague who was my second hire at Dyvintel, my business intelligence firm. We were both excited to reconnect, as it had been years since we'd seen each other. He had worked for me for five years before advancing to increasingly senior roles in data analytics and business intelligence. Over time, he had built an impressive career, and I couldn't have been prouder of his success. As we caught up, he told me he was starting a new venture and wanted me to be part of it. At first, I laughed it off. I hadn't been in the marketplace for so long that I couldn't even imagine how to start again. But he was persistent. He assured me that he'd send me resources to help me catch up with the latest developments in artificial intelligence (AI). He followed through on his promise, but when I started reading the material, it felt overwhelmingly complex. I put it aside, unsure of where to even begin.

Then, a few months later, something happened that changed everything. During our annual summer convention at church, my husband gave me a prophecy—one that left me perplexed. I was expecting a word related to my ministry, but instead, he spoke about God leading me back into the marketplace. I left that meeting confused, unsure of what it meant or what God had in store for me. Part of me resisted this idea. After all, I had stepped away from the marketplace to focus on ministry, and I couldn't imagine returning to a place I had left behind. But I chose to trust God's direction.

One of the biggest reasons for my resistance was the pace at which data analytics, AI, and machine learning had advanced during my time away. I felt daunted by the technological progress that had occurred and intimidated by the idea of having to catch up. I also worried that I might have to start from the bottom, and the thought of that felt humiliating. But, I consecrated myself to God, saying, "I will do what You want for my life." At that moment, I had completely forgotten about the conversation with my colleague about joining his startup.

In the midst of my uncertainty, I decided to take some certifications to help me dive back into the field. I chose courses in cloud computing and other foundational technologies essential to AI. I also enrolled in a course called "Artificial Intelligence for Leaders." As soon as I started studying, I realized it wasn't as difficult as I had imagined. The material came alive, and all my passion for data resurfaced.

Then, one day, while I was studying, I heard God speak to me again. This time, His words were clear and profound: "I asked for your Isaac, and you gave it. And now I am giving it back to you." Those words stopped me in my tracks. Overcome with emotion, I pushed my chair back, dropped to my knees, and laid my face on the carpet of my home office. And I wept.

I didn't cry because returning to the marketplace felt like a promotion. On the contrary, my five years in full-time ministry had shown me how fulfilling it was to give myself wholeheartedly to the work of God. I had grown accustomed to the impact I could make in ministry, and I had settled into it. My tears weren't because I felt that returning to the marketplace was a "better" place. It wasn't. I had been deeply fulfilled by the work I was doing for the kingdom.

No, my tears came from a place of recognition and awe. The tenderness in God's voice, the personal nature of His words, broke me. It wasn't just that He was calling me back to the marketplace; He was acknowledging my sacrifice, my obedience, and the love behind it. His message was clear: "I see you. I love you. Your obedience has been accepted, and now, I am ready to bless you with what's next."

Second, I was in awe that God could be so intentional with my life. Could it be that He had orchestrated every detail of my journey, whether in the marketplace, full-time ministry, or both? Was it possible that God had crafted a master plan for my life, one that I couldn't yet fully comprehend? When I left the marketplace, I never thought of it as giving up an "Isaac." I believed that I was making a permanent move, a shift I would never revisit. But now, in a way that challenged my assumptions, God was showing me that He had simply repurposed that chapter. He wasn't taking something away, but reassigning it. What a humbling realization, to know that I am an instrument in God's hands, ready to be repurposed whenever He needs.

There were times when I prayed, convinced that I was of greater use to God in full-time ministry. On those days when the technical knowledge I needed to catch up on seemed insurmountable, I wondered if returning to the corporate world was the right choice. But a dear friend of mine reminded me that five years before, when God called me from the marketplace to ministry, I had felt the same resistance. God, as always, knew me better than I knew myself. He was showing me that my journey wasn't linear. It was dynamic.

My husband, too, had sensed that I wasn't finished with the marketplace. He had been concerned during my five years in full-time ministry, knowing that I have a deep analytical mindset and a love for technology, particularly anything related to data. He often told me he didn't want me to regret closing the door on the marketplace. So, when the call came to return, he was excited, and his excitement was contagious. He knew this would be a journey full of challenges, but also growth, and he was right, though there have been plenty of uncertainties and hard work along the way.

The skills I developed during my time in full-time ministry have proven invaluable in this new phase of my career. Resourcefulness, honed through managing diverse ministry projects, has helped me navigate the dynamic challenges of the corporate world. Flexibility, developed from adapting to the varying needs of a growing congregation, has enabled me to pivot quickly in the fast-moving world of data analytics and AI. The humility to learn from others, an essential part of ministry, has kept me open to fresh perspectives, fostering continuous growth and innovation. Embracing growth in both my spiritual and professional life has positioned me to approach new technologies and methodologies with confidence. By integrating these leadership skills with my technical expertise, I am able to contribute more effectively and with a renewed sense of purpose.

I am still on this journey, with an open heart and trust in the future God has in His hands. Knowing that He controls my seasons and times, I am confident that everything will fall into place. My goal is to be a thought leader in whatever role God calls me to, helping companies use data to drive organizational growth and make a lasting impact. This journey of faith and obedience has shown me that consecration isn't about giving up parts of your life. It's about embracing God's full plan, trusting that He is always working for our good and His glory.

Five Consecration Lessons from Chapter 10

1. **Obedience in Uncertainty**
   One of the most pivotal lessons in my journey back to the marketplace was learning to obey God's call, even when the path ahead seemed unclear. Transitioning back into the corporate world after years in ministry was a leap into the unknown. But through it, I realized that true consecration is not about sticking to a comfortable, predictable path but about surrendering to God's greater plan, even when it challenges our comfort zones and expectations. It's about trusting that even in uncertainty, His guidance is leading us to something bigger than we could imagine.

2. **Resourcefulness and Adaptability**
   Returning to the corporate world required me to tap into the resourcefulness and adaptability I developed while in ministry. Those years taught me how to manage diverse projects, solve problems creatively, and remain flexible to changing circumstances. Consecration, I learned, is about being ready to pivot to meet God where He's calling, whether that's in ministry or the marketplace. It's about bringing the skills you've gained from every experience into whatever role He places you in, with an open mind and a

heart ready to contribute.

3. **Humility and Continual Learning**

   A key takeaway from my journey has been the importance of humility and a commitment to lifelong learning. My time in ministry taught me to listen actively, learn from others, and lead with empathy. Returning to a fast-paced field like AI and data analytics meant humbling myself and embracing new ideas, technologies, and methodologies. Consecration means remaining open to spiritual and professional growth and being willing to constantly learn, adapt, and refine our skills in service of God's purpose.

4. **Purposeful Repurposing**

   One of the most powerful revelations in my journey was the realization that God can repurpose our experiences for His glory. No season is wasted. The skills and insights I gained in ministry were not left behind but were redirected to fulfill a new purpose. Consecration is about seeing every chapter of our lives as part of God's intentional design. It's about trusting that He has a plan for every experience, whether in the corporate world, in ministry, or anywhere in between, and that each experience prepares us for the next assignment..

5. **Embracing God's Comprehensive Plan**

   Ultimately, the journey has shown me that God's plan for our lives is both comprehensive and beautiful. Whether we are in the marketplace or in ministry, He is always working for our good and His glory. Embracing His plan means trusting that every season, every role, and every shift has purpose. Consecration is about stepping into whatever calling He has for us with confidence, knowing that we are part of a divine purpose that is bigger and more meaningful than we could ever imagine

11

A Call to Consecration

A consecrated career begins with a consecrated life. It's not just about the work we do, but about the purpose we dedicate to it. Everything we offer, whether it's our time, our talents, or our careers, begins with the consecration of our lives to a higher purpose. To consecrate means to devote, hallow, or dedicate—each term signifying a commitment to something greater than ourselves. And when we live with this dedication, our careers follow suit.

God gave us free will. With this freedom, we can choose our paths, but His expectation is clear: He wants us to choose Him, and choose His will for our lives, even when it's difficult. The choices we make aren't always easy. Often, what we want to do and what God wants for us are not aligned. The real challenge of Christian living is choosing to set aside our desires and commit ourselves to what God calls us to do, especially when it seems like a sacrifice.

The world is often in direct opposition to God's will. Every day, we make countless decisions; many of them unconsciously. Those unconscious decisions are shaped by our programming, our biases, and our default settings. A consecrated life, however, involves reprogramming those default settings to align with what God wants. It's about making intentional choices, every day, to serve His greater purpose.

When I moved from California to Chicago to start a church, it was one of the hardest decisions I'd ever made. I left behind a great job and a comfortable life, stepping into the unknown, relying only on God's promises. I felt a deep connection to Abraham, called to leave what was familiar in pursuit of something greater, even though the path was unclear. Abraham's obedience, even when it took years to manifest, was ultimately rewarded. And so, I believed mine would be, too.

I expected that my sacrifice, leaving a great job, would quickly be followed by a new opportunity. But God's timeline was not my own. I wanted a new job, but God wanted something deeper: He wanted a consecrated life. One day, He gave me a vision of my life as a pie, a pizza. The job I wanted was just one slice, but there were other slices that needed to be in place first. He was working on those. The details, the small, often overlooked pieces of my character, needed to be aligned with His will. He was teaching me that consecration doesn't just apply to the big decisions, but to the little things too.

In the waiting season, I learned tough lessons: how to handle jealousy and covetousness, how to trust Him with my finances, and how to become sensitive to His leadings, especially when something didn't feel right. All of this was part of living a consecrated life. I wanted a job, but what God wanted was for me to fully dedicate my life to Him. A job would come, but it would be a reflection of the deeper transformation that was happening within me.

To live a consecrated life, we must recognize that our jobs are from God. It's easy to get swept up in the success and prestige of a career, forgetting that our ability to work, to earn, and to provide is all a gift. I remember the first time I tithed after months of unemployment and seeking a job. Tithing, for me, wasn't about following a rule, it was a reflection of my heart. The first 10 percent of my income, set aside for God's work, was a reminder that everything I had was a gift from Him.

Whether or not you believe tithing is required under the New Testament, what matters is what it does to your heart. It's an act of acknowledgment, an affirmation that all that we have is because of Him. A consecrated life, both in career and giving, is about living with intention, understanding that our work is more than just what we do for a paycheck—it reflects our deeper commitment to a purpose beyond ourselves.

In Deuteronomy 8:11-18, God warned the Israelites that when they entered the promised land, settled down, and enjoyed prosperous lives, they must not forget the Lord who had brought them out of slavery, guided them through the wilderness, and delivered them from many dangers. Despite these warnings, the Israelites repeatedly turned away from God, setting up idols and acting as if their success was solely due to their own efforts. This behavior should serve as both a lesson and a warning to us today. We often fall into the trap of becoming self-focused, especially when things are going well. It's easy to forget how much of our progress, whether in our careers, personal lives, or anything else, has been influenced by God's grace.

How often do we find ourselves thinking, "I'm so bright and skilled," or "I have the right connections"? While it's true that people have played a part in our success, we must remember that God is the one who orchestrates it all. He is the one who gives us the favor and opportunity to thrive. It's easy to overlook God's role, but it's important to recognize that every achievement, every step forward, comes from Him. Even if it's our skills, our hard work, or the relationships we build, none of these would be possible without God's grace. He's the one who gives us breath every day, enabling us to work, think, interact, and perform the tasks that move our careers forward. Each and every part of our professional lives is made possible by the God who created and intricately designed us.

Even if your career is not where you want it to be right now, even if you feel like you're stuck in a wilderness, there is always something to be thankful for. The hope for something better is a gift from God. This hope, the picture of a brighter future, is shaped by the Holy Spirit within us. What if you were completely hopeless? What if you could not see any path forward? It's the grace of God that allows us to maintain hope. Even in tough times, we can thank God for the ability to hope.

Our jobs, our careers, and every good thing we have or hope for are all from God. Every opportunity, every step forward, every new connection, comes from His grace. Psalm 103:1-2 says, "Bless the Lord, O my soul; And all that is within me, bless His holy name! Bless the Lord, O my soul, And forget not all His benefits." And James 1:17 reminds us, "Every good gift and every perfect gift is from above, and comes down from the father of lights, with whom there is no variation or shadow of turning."

A consecrated career is one that acknowledges God every step of the way. It's about recognizing His role in all aspects of your professional life, both the big milestones and the small moments. This practice of gratitude must become a daily habit. We must remember that He gave us the opportunity, the job, the connections, and the talents we have. Don't let His goodness become old or taken for granted. Every success, every opportunity, every advancement in your career—remember, it comes from Him.

You want a fulfilling career, one that promises growth and purpose; this is an admirable goal. But remember, the key is to stay consecrated. Consecration is not just a means to an end. It is both the journey and the destination. Once you achieve the goals you've set for yourself, you will likely face another new journey. The process of consecration doesn't stop once you reach a milestone. There have been many moments in my career when I needed to sacrifice something, whether through direct instruction from God or through actions that required me to let go of parts of my career.

When God called my husband to Chicago to start a church, He didn't directly speak to me at first. He didn't ask me to leave California, nor did He tell me that I was supposed to go to Chicago. But I made a decision based on our shared commitment in marriage and ministry. I reasoned that if God spoke to my husband, He was speaking to me too. I believed in the vision we shared, and I knew my part was to support it. My decision wasn't made out of obligation but out of a deep consecration to the vision God had given us. Even if God hadn't directly spoken to me about Chicago, I was willing to sacrifice my career for something I knew was a higher calling. This was an act of consecration—not just to God, but to my marriage and the ministry we were building together.

Similarly, in 2007, when I faced the decision of whether to continue my long commute to work or relocate, I could have chosen differently. I could have pushed for us to move closer to my job to make things easier. But I knew it would take us farther from the church we had planted, and something had to give. Choosing to let go of that job was difficult, but it ultimately led to an incredible offer; the company I had worked for offered to be my first client if I started my own business. That moment, that choice, came as a reward for my many consecrated acts.

After running my business for ten years, God called me to full-time ministry.

At the time, I wasn't expecting it. I had other plans, prospects for the future, and growth on my mind. Though I had thought about full-time ministry before, it never felt like the right time until God made it clear. Saying yes was an act of obedience, an act of consecration. Saying yes to God, even when I didn't fully understand it, was a test of my trust in His plan. And I said yes.

Consecration, at its core, is about saying "yes" to God, no matter how difficult. It's a commitment to His will, His purpose, even when it's unclear, inconvenient, or challenging. In my experience, God has a grand plan, and I fit into that plan somewhere. The challenge is finding where I fit, while trusting that He will guide me when I need it most.

The journey, both in my career and in life, has never been linear. It's been filled with turns, pauses, and unexpected shifts. There have been moments when my intellect, my plans, and my assumptions made me think I had it all figured out. But I have learned that trusting in my understanding alone won't always get me where I need to go. Instead, I need to allow myself to be neutral, to listen, and to follow God's guidance, even when it doesn't align with my own plans.

A career journey, like the greater journey of purpose, requires sensitivity to God's voice. It's not a straight path, and I must be open to the redirections He provides. Proverbs 3:5 reminds us, "Trust in the Lord with all your heart, And lean not on your understanding." Proverbs 14:12 warns, "There is a way that seems right to a man, But its end is the way of death." These words underscore the importance of not solely relying on our intellect or understanding, but being willing to trust in God's guidance, even when we don't see the full picture.

Consecration is about being willing to follow God's lead, especially when it challenges your understanding or your comfort zone. Trusting God's plan means saying yes, even when you don't know where it will lead.

How do you discern what seems good from what is actually the right path? The answer is through one consecrated act at a time. Consecration isn't just a means to an end. In fact, when you reach what you perceive as the "end," you'll find that there's always more consecration ahead. It's an ongoing journey, not a one-time decision.

God may have already given you a word about the next phase of your life, whether in relationships, career, or purpose. For me, that word came from Mark 10:28, a verse that spoke deeply to my heart. Even though I was leaving a job I loved in California to obey God's call to start a church with my husband in Chicago, I was certain that He would reward my obedience with something even greater in my career. I expected a better job to manifest as the result of my faith and sacrifice.

What I learned, however, was that the reward I received wasn't just for my faith, it was a reward for my consecration. It wasn't the reward I envisioned, but it was undoubtedly the reward God intended. And that reward was good. Consecration brings rewards, but those rewards may not always look the way you expect. Still, they come from God, and that makes them meaningful, fulfilling, and true to His plan for your life.

I've experienced many unexpected rewards in my career; blessings that went beyond anything I could have imagined. After starting Dyvintel, for instance, I was approached by a SaaS company seeking business intelligence consulting services for their customers, primarily in the manufacturing sector. This opportunity exposed me to a new world, working closely with top-level executives at leading companies across the US and Canada. It was a game-changer, expanding my reach and influence in ways I hadn't anticipated.

I vividly remember a week-long engagement where I trained the owner of a chemical manufacturing company in business intelligence. This company was a family-owned business in the $300M to $400M range, a significant player in the American economy. During one of our sessions, the CEO, who was in his late sixties, had a breakthrough moment. As we explored data-driven decision-making, he suddenly exclaimed, "That is what my father saw." Here was a man, decades after his father's vision had been realized, uncovering the power of data to bring that vision to life. It was a humbling, almost divine moment to be part of that process.

Soon, I became the sole business intelligence consultant for this SaaS company, supporting them after their entire BI team had left. As a result, I hired and trained additional consultants. Although we never became a large company, we were agile and known for our innovation and ability to get projects done in the most creative ways.

The Bible teaches that God rewards our secret acts of consecration, those quiet moments of devotion, obedience, and trust. Whether it's private prayer, quiet giving, or fasting in solitude, these acts are not meant for public recognition. Instead, they stem from a sincere heart and a desire to honor God. In our careers, when we trust God for our rewards, we learn to look beyond earthly validation and human accolades, recognizing that our true reward comes from Him.

Consecration brings rewards. Not always the way you expect, but always in a way that serves God's greater purpose for your life. And those rewards, no matter how they appear, are worth every act of obedience and every sacrifice.

12

Heart at Work

Heart issues often profoundly impact every area of our lives, including our careers and our ability to lead consecrated lives within those careers. These internal struggles shape our perceptions, actions, and ultimately our success and fulfillment. Let's explore some of these heart issues and how they can influence both our personal and professional lives.

I remember how embarrassed I used to feel when sharing my resume. My earliest memory of feeling self-conscious about it dates back to when I was at the University of Oklahoma, just before a National Society of Black Engineers (NSBE) conference. I couldn't attend the event, which was held in another state, but a friend of mine was going. He offered to take copies of my resume and submit them to some companies on my behalf. I immediately felt uncomfortable. I didn't want him to see my resume—it didn't reflect much work experience. Meanwhile, he had an impressive resume filled with campus leadership roles, including being a residential advisor, and holding multiple jobs. I was ashamed.

When I handed him my resume, I watched his face, bracing myself for a subtle look of disappointment. But instead, he looked up and said, "Wow, your GPA is amazing!" His response took me by surprise. While I focused on what I thought I lacked, he saw something entirely different. He saw my academic excellence, which I had completely overlooked. Shame made me focus on what I didn't have, while he appreciated what I did.

Let's talk about shame.

Webster's dictionary defines shame as "a painful emotion caused by the consciousness of guilt, shortcomings, or impropriety." Some of its synonyms include discomfort, embarrassment, humiliation, and disgrace, while its antonyms are approval, esteem, honor, praise, and respect. Shame is often not about what others think of us, but about how we feel about ourselves. Our sense of self-worth is deeply tied to our internal beliefs and the way we see ourselves. For many, this perception is rooted in a type of sin-consciousness we inherit that makes us feel inadequate or inferior.

Our background plays a significant role in shaping these feelings. Whether it's economic, racial, or social status, our family histories often shape how we perceive ourselves. For example, someone who grew up in a single-parent household might have always felt "less than" children from two-parent families. This feeling of being "different" might be misinterpreted as inferiority and doesn't necessarily fade with age. Even if they later build a successful family and career, that lingering sense of shame can persist.

I recently spoke to someone who still avoids her high school classmates, even thirty years later, because she grew up in a family that she felt was economically disadvantaged compared to her peers. Despite now being married, having children, and achieving financial stability, she still feels uncomfortable around her old classmates. The stigma from her past continues to influence her, leaving her with a sense of being "less than," even though she's achieved much since then.

This type of shame can limit us in more ways than we realize, affecting both how we see ourselves and how we project ourselves in the workplace and in leadership. It can stop us from fully embracing opportunities or speaking up for what we deserve. It affects how we connect with others, whether we feel worthy to take a seat at the table, or whether we believe that our achievements are valid.

The key to moving past shame is recognizing it for what it is: an emotional barrier that keeps us from seeing our own value and potential. To live a consecrated life in our careers, we must first confront the heart issues, like shame, that try to keep us tethered to past perceptions. This internal work is foundational in helping us step into the fullness of what God has called us to in both our personal and professional lives. We need to redefine our self-worth, not based on past limitations, but on the potential within us, rooted in our identity in God.

By addressing these heart issues, we free ourselves to grow into the leaders we are meant to be. Leaders who are not bound by past experiences but empowered by God's love and purpose for our lives.

We all carry shame, often because of mistakes we've made in the past. These mistakes can seem so large in our minds, lingering far longer than anyone else remembers them. We might hold on to them, letting them shape our self-worth, even after the world has moved on. It's important to remember that everyone makes mistakes. Every successful person has made some foolish choices. You are not the only one who has lost friends, opportunities, or money because of an avoidable error. You know better now and would do things differently if you could. But the reality is, you did the best you could with what you knew at the time. Don't let the shame of ignorance hold you back forever.

There were certainly decisions I made when I was younger that I would approach differently if I had the chance. But I can't turn back time to undo those mistakes. What I can do, however, is make sure that the disappointment or shame of those mistakes doesn't weigh me down and prevent me from reaching toward the bigger opportunities in the future.

Shame often arises when our actions or beliefs aren't aligned with what others expect or agree with. It's easy to shrink back, to conform, and try to blend in. But mavericks don't conform. They embrace their own beliefs and act on them boldly. The safety of conformity often stops people from exploring the ideas and opportunities God has placed in front of them. Shame leads to self-consciousness, which keeps us focused on fitting in, rather than standing out and being true to our unique path.

Another source of shame comes from comparing ourselves to others, especially when we feel we haven't achieved what they have. This is why reunions or family gatherings can sometimes feel uncomfortable. People often compare their own achievements to what their peers have done. When they feel they've fallen short, it triggers feelings of inferiority. That's the core of the inferiority complex: believing we're "less than" someone else.

When I was starting out in my professional career, I was extremely ambitious. My drive led me to make some decisions I later regretted. One in particular caused me shame for a long time. I ran my business intelligence firm for several years, but eventually, our pipeline dried up, and I realized we needed new opportunities. I advised my consultants to seek positions with larger companies doing similar work, and I decided to look for a job myself.

At the time, I was in contact with a project manager at one of our largest clients. I told her I was no longer available for their projects because I was pursuing full-time employment. She immediately urged me not to leave, offering to use her connections to get me hired within the company. She had done a lot for me and my company in the past, and I was grateful for her support. She followed through and secured me a job, although it was not the one I wanted. I was offered a lower position, but she assured me that I would be promoted soon.

Initially, I accepted the role, but disappointment quickly set in. I had expected more, and the promotion wasn't coming as quickly as I'd hoped. When an opportunity arose to work with her boss, I jumped at it. In discussions with him, I told him how much I disliked my current role and how my friend had promised a faster promotion. I didn't consider how this might reflect poorly on her—how she might feel betrayed by me discussing our agreement with her superior. My ambition and impatience clouded my judgment.

I did get the position I wanted, but soon after, the company restructured, and both my boss and I were laid off. My friend, however, was unaffected and even promoted. The irony wasn't lost on me.

While the layoff eventually led to an opportunity that allowed me to restart my company, I carried the shame of my actions for a long time. I had been too driven and too focused on my own ambitions. I hadn't acted with the grace and patience that I now understand is required in leadership. Instead of being patient and letting the fruit of the Spirit guide me, I took matters into my own hands and, in the process, turned a friend and ally into an enemy.

But even that shame was something I had to let go of. I had to recognize that I would have handled things differently if given another chance, and that's part of growth. Consecration involves learning from our mistakes and moving forward, not letting past actions define us. Through reflection and learning, we grow into the leaders we are meant to be, one step at a time.

Shame can be a powerful and tormenting emotion, often holding us back from fully embracing our potential. It can skew our perception of ourselves, magnifying our flaws while diminishing our achievements. When we live with shame, we are often more focused on our perceived deficiencies than our strengths, leading us to overcompensate in areas where we feel inadequate. Yet, the scriptures offer a different perspective on shame, highlighting faith, hope, and love as powerful antidotes.

Romans 10:11 and Psalm 34:5 show us that shame can be overcome when we place our trust in God's promises. Living unashamed is a journey that requires not only confronting our deepest fears but also redefining our self-image through God's love and grace. When we do this, we open the door to living confidently, making decisions rooted in purpose rather than fear, and fully embracing the potential that lies ahead.

The story of Adam, as told in Genesis, serves as a reminder of the origin of shame and the redemptive power of grace. Shame entered the world through sin, but it is through the righteousness and grace we receive from God that we are liberated. In my life, releasing shame meant acknowledging past mistakes, learning from them, and moving forward with a renewed sense of purpose. It meant recognizing that my value is not determined by my achievements, background, or the approval of others, but by my worth as a child of God.

As we navigate our careers and personal growth, we must remember that we are not defined by our moments of shame. Rather, we are defined by our resilience, our capacity for love, and our ability to embrace the limitless possibilities that lie ahead. By shedding the weight of shame, we can step into a future full of joy and opportunity, free from the burdens of the past.

For example, when I look at someone like Elon Musk, I don't feel the need to compare myself. I admire his accomplishments and am inspired by his drive, but I don't feel jealousy or inadequacy. I've never looked at his net worth and felt depressed or disheartened by my own financial standing. This is a mindset I've cultivated throughout my career. It's important to look at others with admiration and inspiration, rather than comparison and envy.

However, imagine this: What if I came across a story online about an old neighbor of mine, someone I hadn't kept in touch with for years? This person, someone who once lived in a less prestigious home than mine, was suddenly featured on Forbes as the wealthiest person in the world. I might begin to feel a sense of discomfort or even jealousy. Why? It's because I perceive a basis for comparison. This person was once close to me—they were a neighbor, perhaps a friend, or a classmate. When we feel there's a direct comparison, we often begin to measure our worth against theirs, and jealousy creeps in.

This is where competitive jealousy comes in. It's an internal indictment that suggests, "If they can do it, why can't I?" It arises from the belief that we must have done something wrong to not have what they have. We might think, "I must not have worked as hard. I must not have been as smart. I must have made mistakes they didn't make." This kind of internal processing can be so subtle that we may not even recognize it. But the feelings are real—an uncomfortable discomfort that arises when we compare our success to someone else's.

Recognizing and addressing these feelings of jealousy is crucial in the journey to living a fully consecrated life. We must confront these moments of comparison and self-doubt with the knowledge that our path is unique, and our success will come in its own time. There is no one-size-fits-all approach to success, and comparing our journey to others only hinders our progress. By focusing on the purpose and calling God has placed in our lives, we can avoid falling into the trap of unhealthy comparisons and instead embrace the unique journey He has set before us.

Competitive jealousy is an emotion that has the potential to consume us, distract us, and hold us back from fully embracing our own journey. At its core, competitive jealousy arises from the feeling of unhappiness or anger when someone else achieves something we desire. But what makes this emotion particularly dangerous is that we often don't even realize that we're jealous until we see someone else with what we think we want. It is only in their success that we become hyper-focused on a goal or achievement we hadn't even previously considered.

The nature of competitive jealousy is flawed and, frankly, ridiculous. We are all unique individuals, each with our own experiences, desires, and paths. Just because we may have shared certain experiences—like attending the same school or working at the same company—does not mean that our journey, goals, or ultimate success should be compared. We all have different motivations, and our paths are not meant to mirror each other. Instead of allowing competitive jealousy to lead us into self-condemnation, we should celebrate others' successes. If an old classmate becomes the VP at a major company, celebrate that fact. Someone had to be that VP, so why not someone you know? There's no need for jealousy, just admiration and appreciation.

At times, competitive jealousy can stem from pride. When someone we perceive as being on a different level from us reaches a milestone we haven't yet achieved, it can trigger feelings of inadequacy. "How could they have achieved that and not me?" we might think. This type of jealousy often arises when we feel like we deserve something that someone else has received. This kind of thought is rooted in pride, and it's important to recognize it. When pride fuels our jealousy, we need to humble ourselves and refocus. A scripture that helps me in these moments is Philippians 2:3: *"Don't be selfish; don't try to impress others. Be humble, thinking of others as better than yourselves."* This mindset shifts our perspective, allowing us to celebrate others instead of competing with them, which strengthens our relationships and fosters an environment of mutual respect.

Another antidote to competitive jealousy is to consecrate ourselves to God and His unique plan for our lives. If recognition, promotions, or accolades are part of His plan for us, great! If not, we can still find joy in the path we're on, knowing that God is with us every step of the way. Whether we're in a valley or on a mountaintop, God's presence is the most important part of our journey. I take comfort in knowing that God has chosen to be involved in my career, transforming what could seem like mundane tasks into opportunities for growth and learning. For me, walking with God is the ultimate reward. I don't need external recognition or praise to be content; His presence in my life is more than enough.

Competitive jealousy can rob us of our gratitude for what we already have. When we get caught up in comparing ourselves to others, we lose sight of our own blessings. Gratitude is the foundation for a fulfilled life, and without it, we diminish the good things already at work in our lives. Moreover, jealousy can distract us from the future God has planned for us. We may miss out on the opportunities in front of us because we're so focused on someone else's success. There is always something we should be working on, something that will lead us to an even greater future, but jealousy blinds us to these possibilities.

Competitive jealousy, if left unchecked, will rob us of life's precious moments. Instead, we should consecrate ourselves to God, focusing so intently on walking with Him that we are not distracted by the accomplishments of others. Consecration is about living with purpose, grounded in the present and trusting that the path God has for us is always leading us toward something greater.

Illusions are beliefs that distort the truth, even if they contain elements of reality. These are the mental constructs we create—whether we overestimate our abilities or underestimate ourselves, whether we inflate our expectations or sell ourselves short. We may feel confident in our abilities, thinking success is guaranteed, only to face rejection after rejection when we try something new. We can even get convinced of something that feels achievable, only to find ourselves struggling with the very task we thought we could easily conquer. The sooner we face these illusions, the sooner we can remove the roadblocks that prevent us from moving toward our real goals.

An illusion, by definition, is a distortion of reality, a false belief or idea. While hope and confidence are essential and positive, when they are based on illusions, they can create significant obstacles in our personal and professional lives. We may believe we are ready for a career shift, only to find that we are not as prepared as we thought. God works in truth, not in illusions. He doesn't want us to be misled about our abilities, where we are, or where we're going. It's essential to face reality and, from that place, start to dream and act with clarity. Confronting reality may not be easy, but it's an essential step for true growth and progress.

Disillusionment is often an uncomfortable experience that crashes into our lives, shaking up the illusions we've held. But, in reality, it's not necessarily harmful. Disillusionment can be a divine invitation to see things more clearly, to shed misconceptions, and embrace the truth of what's really happening in our lives. I believe it's through moments of disillusionment that we are offered the opportunity for transformation. As we face the gap between our expectations and reality, we can choose to allow these moments to refine us, rather than defeat us.

In my journey, disillusionment has been transformative. It has often acted as a refining process, peeling away the illusions I once held, and revealing the truth of my purpose and path. It has reminded me that God's plan for me isn't always how I envision it but is always better than what I could have imagined. I've learned that God's truths are liberating. Jesus said, "If you abide in My word, you are truly My disciples. And you will know the truth, and the truth will set you free." (John 8:31-32). Confronting the truth, however difficult it may seem, opens up a new way of living—one rooted in authenticity and trust in God's timing.

When I think about the moments of disillusionment in my life, I remember the story of the disciples on the road to Emmaus, who were filled with sorrow and confusion after Jesus's death. But in that moment of disillusionment, they encountered the risen Christ. Through their shattered expectations, they were able to recognize the truth of God's presence. This story serves as a reminder that disillusionment, though painful, can lead to a deeper understanding of God's truth and purpose in our lives.

So, how do we navigate these moments of disillusionment? With humility and openness. As we confront the reality of our situations, we need to invite God into that space. His presence brings clarity, peace, and the ability to move forward. Just as Peter experienced in the aftermath of the crucifixion, we are often invited to face our own disillusionments—not with despair but with the hope of transformation. As we acknowledge the truth, we step closer to understanding God's will for us.

The cross itself is the ultimate example of disillusionment. What seemed like the greatest defeat became the most profound victory. Similarly, in our lives, the challenges and setbacks we experience may seem like failures, but they often serve as the foundation for greater success and fulfillment. By walking through disillusionment with God, we allow Him to shape us into who we are meant to be, refining our character and preparing us for the next stage in our journey.

In this chapter, we have explored the profound effects of shame, competitive jealousy, and disillusionment. These heart issues, whether they stem from past experiences, unmet expectations, or false beliefs, can hinder our growth and cloud our vision for the future. However, by confronting them head-on, we have the opportunity to redefine our self-worth and realign ourselves with divine truths. Letting go of shame allows us to see our inherent worth. Overcoming competitive jealousy helps us celebrate others' success without comparison. Embracing disillusionment allows us to remove false beliefs and step into a clearer, more authentic understanding of our purpose.

As we continue our journey of faith and career development, let's remember that a consecrated life—one dedicated to God's purpose—is a life free from the constraints of shame, jealousy, and illusions. Embracing God's plan for our lives helps us overcome these barriers and live with confidence, hope, and resilience. By trusting in His timing and following His direction, we can move forward into a future filled with purpose, growth, and limitless potential.

13

The Christian at Work

In today's fast-paced world, the workplace is where most of us spend the majority of our time. This was a profound realization God brought to my attention several years ago when He gave me a specific assignment about believers in the workplace. He said to me, "How many hours a week do most believers spend in church? Compare that to how many hours they spend at work. I have something to say about that place where they spend most of their time."

Think about it for a moment. On average, most Christians spend anywhere from two to ten hours a week at church, with the more dedicated ones possibly spending more time. But now, compare that to the hours spent preparing for work, commuting, and working itself. For many, we're looking at anywhere from forty to one hundred hours a week. The point here is clear: as a Christian, your faith should be evident at work, where you're spending the majority of your time.

Let's explore a few key aspects of what it means to be a Christian at work:

Integrity: According to the dictionary, integrity is defined as "the quality of being honest and having strong moral principles" and "moral uprightness." At work, you will face situations where pressure may tempt you to compromise on your integrity. You might be presented with an opportunity where doing the right thing could cost you your job, your promotion, or your relationships. This is why it's important to make the decision *beforehand* that you will remain honest, and that you will uphold strong moral principles.

God can guide you out of any situation, even if it means leaving a job that compromises your integrity. Remember, one lie often leads to another. It's easy to get tangled in a web of deceit, but the simplest solution is to be honest from the start. Stick to your principles, be true to your word, and live by the values that reflect your faith.

A powerful example of integrity can be found in 2 Kings 5, where we read the story of Gehazi, a servant to Elisha. Gehazi witnessed his master refuse gifts offered by Naaman, who had been healed of leprosy. However, Gehazi didn't agree with Elisha's decision and decided to act on his own. He secretly met Naaman on the way and told him a fabricated story, convincing Naaman to give him the gifts that Elisha had refused.

Gehazi didn't just deceive Naaman, but also brought Elisha's integrity into question. When Elisha confronted Gehazi, he revealed that the Spirit of God had shown him everything that had happened. Gehazi's dishonesty led to the tragic consequence of him becoming leprous, the very condition Naaman had been healed from.

This story serves as a reminder that as Christians, we must not fall into the temptation to behave like Gehazi at work. It's easy to get caught up in the schemes of others who may be cutting corners or being dishonest. But just because others around you are taking shortcuts doesn't mean you should follow suit.

While you may not face the same consequences as Gehazi, dishonesty at work will affect your conscience. It will dull your sensitivity to God's voice, and over time, it will make it harder for you to hear the Holy Spirit's gentle promptings. The more you ignore His guidance, the harder it becomes to discern right from wrong, and your heart becomes hardened against God.

Consecration at work is about honoring God with your actions, decisions, and relationships. It's about being a person of integrity and setting a standard for others to follow, even when it's challenging. By doing so, we become a light in the workplace, reflecting the love and righteousness of Christ in everything we do.

Integrity is essential for a Christian at work, as it shapes not just your reputation but the witness of your faith in a professional setting. When you approach your work with honesty and adhere to strong moral principles, you align your actions with your values. However, integrity alone will not sustain your career. Hard work, dedication, and a willingness to continuously improve are just as crucial.

A personal story stands out to me when I reflect on the importance of hard work. There was a time early in my career when a recruiter called to let me know that a company had chosen to hire me despite my lack of certain required skills. I was overjoyed and grateful to God because I knew that securing the job was a miracle. However, I also knew that while a miracle got me in, hard work would be needed to remain there. I didn't assume that the job would simply work out for me because of divine favor; I took it upon myself to prepare and to deliver excellence.

Before even starting, I spent sleepless nights studying everything I could about the role. I learned everything I could through the night for several days, knowing that if I were to thrive, I had to work just as hard as God had worked for me. It was important to not just rely on the miracle of getting the job but also to put in the effort that would ensure I stayed and excelled.

Many Christians mistakenly believe that prayers and favor are enough to succeed in their careers. While both are crucial elements, they are not substitutes for diligence. It's essential to remember that God does not reward laziness. Yes, favor can distinguish you, and prayer is vital, but it's your hard work, commitment, and willingness to go above and beyond that will set you apart in your career.

The Bible offers clear guidance on this:

> "He who has a slack hand becomes poor, But the hand of the diligent makes rich. He who gathers in summer is a wise son; He who sleeps in harvest is a son who causes shame." - **Proverbs 10:4-5 NKJV**
>
> "The appetite of the sluggard craves and gets nothing, but the appetite of the diligent is abundantly supplied." - **Proverbs 13:4 AMPC**

When God directs us to work, He isn't calling us to take shortcuts or to hope for an easy path. We must prepare for work to require effort. If it comes easily, that's a blessing, but we shouldn't expect everything to be smooth sailing. Whatever you do, do it with all your might. Be diligent, be the first to arrive at the office and the last to leave. Excellence comes from doing your best, every time, no matter the task.

The rewards of diligence are substantial. Those who are willing to go the extra mile, who stay longer, work harder, and seek out more opportunities, often seem "luckier" than others. But luck isn't what drives them. They are simply aligning themselves with the principles that lead to success.

Early in my career, I discovered a secret to distinguishing myself quickly at a new job. The key was simple: finish the task at hand as quickly as possible and then ask for more responsibilities. Continuously asking for more work and demonstrating your appetite to do more will eventually get you noticed. It was this very mindset that led me to innovate in my first job.

I was tasked with a responsibility that had previously been my boss's—laying out test boards for programmable logic devices. After a while, I began thinking about ways I could improve the process and make it more efficient. I researched the task, and soon I had written a program that could automate the layout process. What used to take me several weeks, I was now able to complete in five days. This innovation not only made my job easier but also significantly improved the efficiency and accuracy of my department.

That innovation wasn't born from a desire to make things easier for the sake of ease. It came from my drive to do more, to work faster, and to contribute more. When we are diligent and committed to excellence, we often find ourselves stumbling upon solutions that make a greater impact than we initially imagined.

Laziness can hinder your progress, but hard work significantly contributes to it. This simple truth is something we all understand intuitively, but putting it into practice is what separates the dreamers from the achievers.

Profitability, by definition, refers to the degree to which an activity or business generates a financial gain. However, profitability isn't solely about money. It's about the sustainable outcomes of your efforts. Not every endeavor will lead to profit, but it's crucial to identify those that have the potential to yield substantial returns. It's not about an obsession with wealth but about ensuring that what you pour your time, energy, and resources into will sustain and support the lifestyle you want to create.

When I raised my children, I didn't dictate their career paths or dictate what they should study in college. Instead, I gave them this advice: whatever you choose to study, make sure it can sustain the lifestyle you want after you graduate. That was a bit of humor, of course, but there was a point to it. I didn't want them living at home indefinitely! The key takeaway is that career decisions need to be based on practicality and profitability, especially when it comes to sustaining long-term success.

There's a particular story that sticks with me. A friend of mine, back in the day, had a boyfriend who planned to drive trucks after college to pay off his student loans. Despite being in the middle of his degree, he already knew that the degree he was pursuing would not be profitable enough to manage his debt. I thought, "If driving a truck would be more profitable, why not just do that from the start?" Why take on debt for a degree that doesn't lead to a profitable career? While some might disagree with this approach, my thinking has remained the same. Whatever you do in your career, always have profitability in mind.

That being said, there are seasons of sacrifice along the journey. Sometimes, you invest significant time, effort, and resources without immediate returns. That's okay, as long as it's part of a well-planned strategy with a clear end goal in mind. But if those sacrifices stretch beyond their season, it may be time for an exit strategy.

For some, entrepreneurship is a calling. But it's not for everyone. I've seen many people who, rather than remaining in paid employment, jumped into entrepreneurship with the wrong expectations. The truth is that not everyone is naturally wired for entrepreneurship, and sometimes staying in a stable job is the smarter choice. If you've jumped into business but realize it's not for you, don't feel trapped. Just make the course correction, find a job that aligns with your skills, and create a steady income. It's never too late to reassess and realign.

The Bible often speaks to us about being fruitful and multiplying, not just in terms of our faith but in all areas of life, including our careers. Jesus uses the parable of the unprofitable servant to highlight the importance of being productive and making the most of the resources we've been given. While the parable addresses the kingdom of God, we can draw valuable lessons about being productive in all areas of our lives, including our professional endeavors.

Don't be an unprofitable Christian, and don't be unprofitable in your career. Aim for growth, increase, and multiplication. Be fruitful in what you do, whether it's your job, your business, or the way you steward your gifts. Stay committed to making a positive impact through your work, always with an eye toward productivity, progress, and sustainability.

Competence, as defined by Dictionary.com, is "the ability to do something successfully or efficiently." In Proverbs 22:29 AMPC, it's written: "Do you see a man diligent and skillful in his business? He will stand before kings; he will not stand before obscure men." The Bible emphasizes the importance of being highly skilled in your work, and this principle holds true in our careers today.

As Christians, we are called to do our work with excellence. We are not called to be just "good enough." Competence is about getting things done efficiently, professionally, and with timeliness. It means being able to rise above the average and stand out in a crowded field. An incompetent person, no matter how well-intentioned, will find themselves replaced by someone more competent. The marketplace rewards competence—competence that translates into value, reliability, and the ability to deliver results.

Competence isn't a static trait; it's tied to capacity development. Without ongoing development, even the most competent individual can fall behind. As industries evolve and technology advances, failing to keep up means your knowledge will become outdated. You need to continually enhance your skills through courses, books, certifications, or just staying updated with trends in your field. Never become comfortable with stagnation. True competence means always striving to be better and doing more.

The story of Daniel and his three friends, Shadrach, Meshach, and Abednego, demonstrates this principle of excellence and competence. These four young men, despite being in a foreign land under difficult circumstances, excelled in a royal training program in Babylon. They were chosen for their inherent qualities, but they didn't stop there but gave themselves fully to the process. They didn't compromise on their values but excelled in knowledge and skill. By the end of the program, they were found to be "ten times better" than their peers. This is the kind of excellence we should strive for in our own careers. As believers, we must aim to learn, grow, and remain exceptional in our respective fields.

Competence is not just about what we already know; it's about our willingness to keep learning. Teachability is an essential quality that every professional should possess. The dictionary defines teachability as "being capable of being instructed." A person who is unteachable is, in essence, a proud person who believes they know it all. But no one knows everything. No matter how successful or experienced we become, we can always learn something new, whether it's a fresh perspective, an innovative idea, or an improvement in a process.

We all have to grow, and growth only happens when we remain open to learning. To be teachable means being humble enough to admit that we don't have all the answers. It means listening, asking questions, and seeking advice from those around us, regardless of their position or experience. Learning doesn't happen only from those in positions of authority; sometimes, the most valuable lessons come from unexpected places.

In summary, being a Christian in the workplace is about embodying key virtues: integrity, hard work, profitability, competence, and teachability. These principles do not just enhance our careers but reflect our dedication to living consecrated lives. Our work becomes a platform for us to demonstrate our faith, uphold moral principles, and pursue excellence.

As we navigate the challenges and opportunities of our careers, we must remember that our work is an extension of our faith. Our actions, our attitudes, and our integrity at work speak volumes about who we are as followers of Christ. Through our work, we can glorify God, influence those around us, and make a meaningful impact in the marketplace. So let us strive for excellence in all that we do, knowing that through our competence and teachability, we can fulfill our calling and honor God in every sphere of life.

14

Conclusion

As we close this book, I hope you've felt both seen and inspired walking through my career journey with me. More than anything, I hope you've come away with this one truth: God can be trusted with every part of your life, including your career. You don't need to compartmentalize your faith or keep certain parts of your story hidden. God already sees your thoughts, your decisions, your ambitions, and your aspirations. He knows the plans He has for you, and how your own plans either align with or drift away from His. That's why consecration has been the thread running through every chapter of this book.

Consecration doesn't mean giving up ambition. It means surrendering it. It means holding your career with open hands, allowing God to guide you where He sees best, even when the road ahead feels unclear. Think of consecration as putting your gear in neutral, letting God steer. Because when we hold too tightly to our own plans, we risk missing the greater story He's writing.

And there is reward in that surrender. Miracles lie in wait on the road of obedience. But miracles alone aren't enough—we also need to develop habits and character that anchor us in the workplace. Qualities like:

Integrity – Be who you say you are, whether the room is full or empty. Let people say, "That person is different." Not perfect, but consistent. Trustworthy. Grounded.

Hard Work & Diligence – Miracles can open doors, but hard work keeps you in the room. Excellence is your responsibility. Show up prepared. Show up strong.

Profitability – It's not enough to work hard; we need to be strategic. Profit matters—spiritually, professionally, and practically. We are called to be fruitful and multiply, in every sense of the word.

Competence and Capacity Development – Never stop learning. Don't settle for "good enough." Stretch. Grow. Seek out the mentors, the books, the courses. And never assume you've arrived.

Teachability – Growth demands humility. It's the posture that says, "I don't know everything—and that's okay." Teachable people are adaptable, open, and always improving.

Shame. Jealousy. Illusion. Disillusionment. These aren't just emotions; they're potential roadblocks. They cloud judgment, fuel comparison, and slow down progress. Consecration clears the clutter of the heart so we can move forward with clarity and courage.

A consecrated career doesn't mean giving up on success. It means defining success on God's terms, not the world's. It means enjoying the ride, even when it's uphill, because you know who's in the driver's seat. For me, consecration rewrote everything: from Silicon Valley to Chicago, from business to ministry, and back to the marketplace. In each phase, I've seen the hand of God honor obedience in unexpected, extraordinary ways.

So now, let me ask you—what will you do differently? How will you start seeing your work not just as a job, but as a calling? A platform. A legacy.

Are you in the right role? In the right place? Are you asking God those questions, or are you avoiding them? Consecration starts with asking the hard things. And then having the courage to say "yes" when the answers stretch you.

God is faithful. He doesn't abandon the people who trust Him. What feels like sacrifice today often becomes testimony tomorrow. You cannot outgive Him. Give Him your career, your decisions, your uncertainties, and watch Him turn it into something more beautiful than you imagined.

This is your one life. Use it wisely. Use it well. And above all, use it in partnership with the One who designed it. Your career can be so much more than a ladder. It can be a legacy.

I'm rooting for you. I'm cheering you on. And I can't wait to hear your consecration story one day.

Acknowledgements

First, I thank God for the story, the journey, and the grace that made this book possible. His mercies in my career have been abundant and undeniable.

To my husband, Kayode Ijisesan—thank you for believing in me before I had the words to express my vision. Your faith and love have anchored every part of this journey.

To my children, Tolu and Temi, your patience, joy, and quiet strength inspire me daily.

To my parents, whose legacy of hard work and faith shaped who I am today, and to my siblings, thank you for always reminding me that excellence runs deep in our bloodline.

Special thanks to my uncle and aunt, Isaac and Alice Olorunnisomo, for welcoming me to America and laying the foundation for my early success.

I am deeply grateful to my writing coach, Laju Iren, and my publishing collaborators, including Funke Afolabi-Brown, Temi Ijisesan, and Tope Adewale. Thank you for bringing skill, heart, and patience to this project.

To the KingsWord family, especially our Chicago community—you are more than a church; you are my home. Thank you for your unwavering support.

To my launch team, mentors, colleagues, and friends—you pulled up chairs for me at tables I might never have reached on my own. Thank you.

And finally, to every reader holding this book: may these pages remind you that your voice matters, and you belong in every room destiny calls you into.

About the Author

May (Mayowa) Ijisesan is a technologist with over two decades of experience spanning Silicon Valley, global nonprofits, and ministry strategy. A graduate of the University of Oklahoma and Cornell University, she currently serves as Executive Vice President of Strategy at KingsWord Ministries International and sits on the advisory board of an AI startup. She is a recipient of the Corporate Excellence Award at the Global Entrepreneurship Festival of Africa. She is Married to Kay Ijisesan, and they have two children, Tolu and Temi.

https://www.LinkedIn.com/in/mayowaijisesan
https://www.instagram.com/mayijisesan
https://www.x.com/mayijisesan
https://www.dearpastorswife.org

Other Books by Mayowa Ijisesan
Wisdon for the Workplace
The Supernatural Woman
Dear Pastor's WIfe

www.ingramcontent.com/pod-product-compliance
Lightning Source LLC
LaVergne TN
LVHW051524070426
835507LV00023B/3283